The
QUICK
Motivation
Method

Q The QUICK Motivation Method

How to make your employees
happier, harder working, and
more productive

Thomas L. Quick

St. Martin's Press   New York

Library of Congress Cataloging in Publication Data

Quick, Thomas L
  The Quick motivation method.

  1. Employee motivation. I. Title.
HF5549.5.M63Q5   658.3'14   79–26820
ISBN 0–312–66062–6

To the memory of Anthony L. Quick

Contents

1. The key to successful management

Why should you want to read this book?

Because you are looking for greater productivity in your work force. You would like to increase the efficiency of the people who report to you, to help them to get more of the results you want more often. That is, you would like them to spend more time and more energy on the tasks that you assign them and on the functions of their positions. Furthermore, you would like their performance of those tasks and functions to meet your standards and the needs of the organization. You might even hope that your subordinates would become more enthusiastic about the work, more committed to achieving those goals that take priority with you. In short, you would like your subordinates to be more effective on the job.

One key to effective performance is simply—but not simplistically—motivation.

Even the newest and least experienced manager realizes that employees who want to do a good job usually produce more and better than those who don't. Where people are genuinely committed to accomplishing organizational objectives, there is often a corresponding low rate of absenteeism and turnover, those familiar dollar drains.

That is why the motivation of employees is the number one concern of professional managers, according to surveys of executives conducted through the years by The Research Institute of America. A sales manager complains that one of his people, an experienced representative, knocks off two or three times a week before three o'clock to play golf or tennis. A vice president worries about her manager of manufacturing support services, a man who knows almost everything there is to know about his job but who runs a sloppy operation and takes two-hour lunches every day.

An office manager is baffled by her secretary who leaves a nearly finished urgent letter in her typewriter at the end of the day. And there is probably no manager alive who isn't faced with an aging employee who has begun to coast through the years remaining until retirement age (which has now been pushed back to seventy).

These are employees who know what to do, and they seem to have the knowledge and the skills to do it well. But they fall short of working up to their potential. They don't put out the effort to do the job as it should be done.

On the other hand, there are employees who exert a great deal of energy. They are active and busy, but their effectiveness is low. What results from all that busyness is disappointing, in both quantity and quality. Such ineffectiveness can be very expensive.

What makes the issue of motivation even more complicated for managers is the change that occurs in people. The forces in a person that make him or her want to do a good job this year may not be the same next year. The ambitious salesman who has always begun his selling day before eight in the morning suddenly reaches a plateau. He shortens his working day and makes fewer calls, much to his manager's chagrin and bafflement. The conscientious supervisor who has always spent much of her time out on the floor with workers, involving herself with everything that went on, now spends more time at her desk, seemingly withdrawn, and calls in sick with disturbing frequency. Very often, though, the change in commitment, in motivation, takes place slowly, and the manager may not be aware of the problem until the employee has lost much of his or her effectiveness in doing the job.

Clearly, monitoring motivation in employees is a high priority task for managers, since motivation is so closely linked to output productivity, lower costs, and higher profits.

There is a personal reward for you, the manager, when your subordinates are highly motivated. The job of managing is a lot easier and more enjoyable when people in a work group are motivated than when they are not. They are pulling in the same direction, voluntarily, without your prodding, pushing, and punishing. People arrive on time, put in a fair day's work, and leave feeling good about what they have done. When they do their work right, they leave time for you to do more of the things you like to do—things that can advance you, the department, and your career—and those functions that *only* you can do, such as planning, coordinating, budgeting, and so on.

But whether people in a work group are strongly motivated or not depends largely upon the management they have. That fact, unfortunately, all too often is obscured. When motivation is low, managers have a tendency to blame poor work attitudes among employees, to characterize subordinates as lazy or disloyal. They talk about low morale. Probably morale *is* low. Employees aren't any happier about the situation than management is. However, management has much more power to do something about the situation than employees have. As a manager, you cannot, strictly speaking, motivate another person. But there is no question about your ability to unblock, enhance, and strengthen the motivating forces within that person.

That's why you are reading this book—to sharpen your ability to manage employees' motivation.

A practical guide

This book has been designed as a practical guide. It is a how-to book. I am concerned primarily with providing guidelines and recommendations that can help you get more of the results you want from the work of others. Theory is, of course, extremely important, and this book is based on what I have found to be sound theory. But, even more important, I believe that when you finish the last chapter you will feel that you have increased both your competence and your confidence. When you put this book down, you should be immediately able to put many of its recommendations into practice.

You will find that some of the theories and techniques described are already familiar to you. You practice some of them now. What is important is that you see how your techniques of motivation management fit together as part of an ongoing system. When you help employees to set goals, when you appraise them, give them feedback, reward them, you seem to be performing certain discrete activities. But you will be more effective if you keep in mind how each of those management functions relates to all of the others. While I'm confident that this book can help you to develop better ways to accomplish many of the management tasks you are already doing, I am convinced that the greatest value to you is the recognition and adoption by you of the *system* of management motivation that I describe. The approach to management of motivation that I demonstrate has been thoughtfully and painstakingly put together and tested in the many years I have been counseling managers as a member of the professional staff of The Research Institute. This approach gets results—but only when applied in a consistent, conscientious manner.

Emphasis on behavior

Because this book emphasizes the practical more than the theoretical, it will be concerned with behaviors more than attitudes. Behavior is something you can see and measure. You know when you have influenced another person to act in a certain way. You may or may not influence another's attitude. Even if you do, you can't always be sure that you have.

To be more precise, this book will deal with *voluntary* behavior. When I talk about motivation, I am referring to voluntary behavior. Motivated behavior is that over which a person has some control. It involves choosing one course of action over another. You, the manager, can provide employees with choices. You can also take steps to make one course, one choice, more desirable to—and more doable for—the employee than another. And if that choice of behavior helps you to accomplish your objectives in a more effective manner, then your motivation management is successful.

I include psychological mind-sets in the category of voluntary behavior. We often develop patterns and habits to such an extent that we perform actions without thinking about them. If you drive to work regularly, you've probably had the experience of becoming aware along the way that you had taken your usual route without making a conscious choice. You were thinking about something else and the streets or roads were selected unconsciously. The conscious choice of the route was made some time ago. But sets and habits can be changed. New choices can establish new patterns of behavior.

Involuntary behavior, such as that rooted in addiction, severe neurosis, and psychosis, cannot be dealt with in this book. Motivation theory described in this book does not cover it and you will probably have little influence over it.

How you see subordinates

While the emphasis in this book is on the behavior of others, something needs to be said about attitude—*yours*. An important consideration is how you look at people. If you convey the message, "I'm OK, you're OK," as Transactional Analysis puts it, your chances of influencing employees' behavior and motivation will certainly be better than if you show suspicion and suggest your own superiority. There must be trust between managers and employees. The manager who conveys the expectation to employees that he or she believes they want to commit themselves to a worthwhile task, job, or career, that they would prefer doing a good job to a poor one, has a better chance of getting that commitment and that good job than a manager who suggests the opposite.

Everyone wants to win—again, in the Transactional Analysis sense. I want to be what I am capable of being, without depriving others of the same chance. I want to do what I am capable of doing, without getting in others' ways. That's winning—if you can be and can do. The I'm-OK-You're-OK manager says, in effect, "I want to win. I know you want to win. And we can both help each other to do just that." The essential message is that we can both accomplish what we want.

A profound respect for the individual is essential for effective motivation management. Managers often bemoan that their subordinates are not more like themselves. In fact, some managers insist upon projecting their own values onto employees: "This is what appeals to me; it should appeal to them." That approach works no more often than does an attempt to control the behaviors of others. You have the ability to influence choices. When you try to control them, you reduce motivated behavior. Controlled employees perform under duress.

These, then, are key words: trust, respect, and results. Results or objectives are what you seek. Results are what employees work for as well.

As you read this, you are no doubt saying, "Yes, I believe that." But more important, are you conveying this message to employees? The approach to motivation management in the following chapters will help you to say it in unmistakable terms. And you may be pleasantly surprised to find that your expectations of better performance will play a part in getting you just that.

Five premises

Certain premises underlie this book. Think about them, accept them, or at least keep them in mind as you read the following chapters. Everything this book has to say about motivation techniques is built on the base formed by the following statements. They are, in my judgment, managerial facts of life.

1 *People have reasons for what they do.* They have goals or objectives, and they choose among them. People do not act blindly. Behavior, as the psychologist would say, does not take place in a vacuum. It is directional. Of course, while it is true that people have reasons for doing what they do, that does not necessarily mean that other people find the behavior reasonable. When I don't understand or sympathize with why another person makes a particular choice of behavior, I must not jump to the conclusion that the person has not made a choice.

As I write this chapter, I sit at my desk on a sunny Saturday morning in July. My window overlooks a park. People are strolling, enjoying the greenery. Others are getting into cars to go to the country or the beach. Still others are on their way to stores to do some shopping. And a few are obviously dressed to play tennis. They have made choices, just as I have. I choose to sit here, writing this book. I have a goal that involves this book. My reward for which I work will be its completion and publication. I will then, as the psychologist would say, be reinforced. Thus, when I act, I do so for a particular goal, objective, reward, or reinforcement.

2 *Whatever people choose to do, they do it to gain something they believe is good for them.* Not only is behavior directed toward a goal, that goal must be seen by the doer as good, something that contributes to the welfare of the person accomplishing the task. It has a value. This is where people often get stalled, because they see other people pursuing goals that do not seem good. Les seems always to say or do things that his boss regards as put-downs. Les's co-workers ask, "Can't he see what damage he's doing himself?" The gratification that Les is enjoying from behavior that others find mystifying overrides the negative consequences. He continues to tweak his boss's nose.

I referred to the reason or goal behind an act as a reward or reinforcement. For the purposes of this book they mean the same thing. I do something, or a series of things, and get rewarded. I do an outstanding job of selling, and I feel a surge of pride. Perhaps my manager offers me a promotion. Or I sit at a table turning out lots of units, and since I am on piecework, I receive more money. I am rewarded. My behavior, in psychological terms, is reinforced. I am not only rewarded for past behavior, but I am also encouraged to repeat that kind of behavior (so long as I continue to want the kind of reward it brings me). The reward needn't be tangible; it may be psychological, like the pride I mentioned above.

As we shall see in depth later, when choosing one course of action over another, I will tend to choose the reward or reinforcer that is most valuable to me, *all other things being equal.*

Incidentally, some managers, in assigning a task, seem to object to an employee's asking, "What's in it for me?" But if you asked yourself the same question when you began to read this book, perhaps next time you can be a bit more tolerant of other people's expressions of self-interest.

3 *Whatever goal I choose has to be attainable.* People do not choose a course solely because it is valuable to them. They have to feel that they actually have a chance to gain it. Most people, no matter how valuable a goal might be to them, won't make the effort to go after it if they believe the chances of obtaining it are slim. The supervisor in production may fantasize about being corporate president, but she won't do anything about it since she believes her education and background are inadequate for reaching that high level.

I can be told that a job with much responsibility and a good income awaits me. All I have to do is to get my advanced degree, something that will involve my going to school three nights a week for three years. I'd like to have the job, but I know that my interest won't be sustained through all of those years of classes. The goal has value, but the probability of reaching it is low.

Incidentally, gamblers provide an exception to this principle. They will pursue a reward that is very remote in attainability. That's why some behavior seems based on what some people call the gambler's fallacy—big payoff but small probability.

Theoretically, a manager ought to be able to predict how an employee will perform a task or job so long as the manager has an idea of the relative value of the reward to the subordinate and the amount of confidence he or she has in getting it done. In other words, task A offers more reward and seems easier to do than task B; therefore the manager could reasonably expect the employee to choose task A. But anything that simple would not require an entire book to explain it. Practically speaking, we are not yet at a point where we can confidently predict other people's behavior. We do, however, know how to build more value into the work, and we can take steps to increase the probability in the person's mind that he or she can obtain the reward.

4 *The conditions under which the job is done can affect its value to the employee or his or her expectations of success.* The situation surrounding the work can change the value of the goal or reinforcer. To illustrate: I have been told that, because of the excellent job I've done as assistant branch manager, I can expect to have my own branch very soon. And soon it comes. But to my great distress I'm going to have to relocate in a sparsely populated part of the mountain West, far away from what I consider to be the mainstream. I may not turn down the promotion, but there's little question that the geographical location and the character of the town have substantially lessened the value of the promotion to me.

People are part of what we call the situation. One of your assistants is an intelligent, experienced specialist in distribution. You hand her what you think is a plum —three months in San Francisco at company expense. She'll be heading up a task force that will design more efficient warehousing and distribution on the West Coast. The rewards are not only immediate—the work is obviously something she is capable of doing, and she will be highly visible as a result of this special duty. But then you tell her to whom she'll be reporting: the Western regional vice-president. His reputation is widely known: In general, he doesn't think women have any business on the corporate scene other than as secretaries; and in particular, he has shown special hostility toward your assistant.

Is the job valuable? Of course. Is success probable? She doesn't know. But she suspects she is in for a rough time. Whatever she does or recommends has a slim chance of being taken seriously. Her expectations of success as task force director are lowered because of the difficult reporting relationship.

5 *You, the manager, can increase the value of the goal, the employee's expectations of reaching it, and enhance the situation surrounding the performance.*

This is really the essence of the book. It isn't, after all, sufficient to know what motivation is, how people behave and why. You need to know that you can influence their choices of behavior. And *how* you can influence them. What you say and do can increase the rewards or reinforcers. For example, you can show how the successful performance of an assignment will enhance the employee's feeling of professional growth and development. Or you can hold out the promise of the external rewards, such as money or promotion, for doing a good job.

There are any number of types of resources that you can provide to help the employee to do a better job and to improve the probability of success in the mind of the subordinate. For example, by arranging special training or equipment or assistance, you can persuade the employee that the job is doable after all. And you are usually in a position to help adjust the situation surrounding the doing—by improving the environment, assigning the right people, setting time schedules to relieve pressure, etc.

In short, the manager can play a major role in the motivation of subordinates to work better. The manager is a key to the deeper commitment of employees to the manager's own—and the organization's—goals.

Every successful manager has to recognize that a large part of that success is due to the performance of subordinates. And the quality of that performance is related largely to the effectiveness of the manager's motivation management techniques. There's little question that a manager can leave subordinates to work disappointingly, or help them to perform outstandingly.

2: Motivation half-truths and half-solutions

How many times have you heard the question, "What do you do with employees who just aren't motivated?"? It's something that many managers ask frequently—in my judgment, too many managers and too frequently. I don't waste time wondering why employees are not motivated, because I know they are. I'm curious about where their motivating forces are working. And their managers should be curious, too.

Often the best efforts of employees are expended off the job. They don't get what they want at work. Sometimes, regrettably, people expend their energies in counterproductive ways on the job. In many cases these people are frustrated by a management that does not understand their need to be given the opportunity and the resources to do the job that they would like to do— and that they are capable of doing.

Referring to people as unmotivated is one of the traps managers frequently fall into. There is no such thing as an unmotivated person—except a dead one. When a manager complains that subordinates are not motivated, he or she is really saying that they don't seem to want to do what the manager wants them to do. That is something quite different. But the trap is more than semantic. The manager who sees employees as being either motivated or unmotivated may be turning a back on responsibility (as well as opportunity). The manager may be convinced that there is nothing he or she can do.

To illustrate: an experienced manager described to me the effectiveness of one subordinate she regarded as highly motivated. After talking at length about the work he was doing that gave her satisfaction, she said something quite remarkable: "Of course, I can't take credit for his good performance." I knew that she had created the kind of work environment in which this subordinate could achieve his personal goals through working to accomplish hers and those of the organization. It was a good match, for which both were responsible. At least, I thought so. I couldn't understand why she refused to accept credit.

Then I remembered that she also declined to accept any responsibility for failures in her department. A manager who is reluctant to take credit for an employee's success may also be trying to find a way to refuse to take blame for another employee's failure. It's true that there are cases in which the manager should take neither. Most times, however, managers must accept the fact that they are a substantial influence in the success or failure of employees.

But, of course, when a manager takes credit, it should be for something specific. The manager who oversees the work of effective subordinates and who says, "Whatever I'm doing, something must be right," isn't likely to learn very much—and may, in fact, not be doing that much right. This manager's success is due more to luck than skill and can vanish at any time.

Another misdirected question that managers often ask is, "How do I motivate my people?" The proper answer to this question is, "You don't." Motivation comes from within the individual. It is not something that one person does to another. What a manager must do is find ways to enhance and reinforce the motivating forces within the employee.

If people talk enough about motivating others, they may actually try to do it—or believe they are actually doing it. At the least, speaking of motivation as some-

thing done to others perpetuates the myth. Furthermore, employees, hearing their boss talk in terms of
motivating them, may worry about being manipulated
rather than motivated.

Other half-truths

Seeing motivation as something that is either there or
not there, or as something that the well-meaning manager does to a subordinate, are only two of the miscon-
ceptions managers express on the subject. Another frequently encountered half-truth is that motivation
applies to groups rather than to individuals. The surge
of interest by managers in motivation theory encourages this, chiefly because most such theory has tended
to stop at defining why *people* in certain categories
behave as they do under certain circumstances. For example, when one talks of categories of human needs, it
is easy to think of categories of people who have those
needs. The vital step of applying theory to individuals is
too often missing. Indeed, it is often impossible.

But another reason why managers may be fond of
thinking about motivation of groups is that it seems
much easier to deal with people than persons. Or at least
that's the way managers sometimes feel. It's difficult
enough to think of managing a work group of fifteen or
twenty. To have to find ways to help each person of that
group to be effective is a formidable consideration. But
that is necessary if a manager is going to have a highly
productive department. Of course, a lot of managers
settle for less. They have to, if they treat everyone essentially the same.

Charisma is sometimes mentioned as the factor that
makes a truly good leader. Charisma can help, if you
have it. Unfortunately, relatively few people have it,
and I don't know how one develops it. But I know that
it exists. Even as a teen-aged boy in military school, I
was in awe of boys only sixteen and seventeen years old

who could induce an unruly group of adolescents to behave in a disciplined manner. These young student officers had built-in or natural leadership qualities. They had charisma.

Fortunately for all of us disadvantaged people without charisma, most managers are made, not born. And the most comfortable aspect of that truth is that nearly anyone can become an effective manager. It doesn't take charisma to get a job well done. Charisma admittedly is or can be effective in crises, when massive work has to be done in a short period of time, when almost superhuman challenges must be faced. But even a charismatic manager may not be very effective in dealing with everyday, mundane sorts of tasks. Besides, charisma has a very personal, maybe even irrational appeal. After all, Hitler was considered a charismatic figure.

Theory X

There are some managers who take what I consider to be the wrong kind of credit for the success of their work group. What these managers are saying is that, without their constant vigilance and efforts, their employees would do nothing. This attitude is a holdover from the days of the Garden of Eden. Adam and Eve were driven out of the garden to work, and work became interpreted as a sort of punishment for sin. Understandably no one —except masochists—enjoys punishment. It is something to be avoided. Therefore, this kind of thinking goes, people traditionally avoid work.

The late social psychologist Douglas McGregor expressed this "traditional" view of people at work—or rather at the avoidance of it—in what he termed Theory X, which is a set of assumptions some managers make about their subordinates:

> The average human being has an inherent dislike of work and will avoid it if he can.

Because of this human characteristic of dislike of work, most people must be coerced, controlled, directed, threatened with punishment to get them to put forth adequate effort toward the achievement of organizational objectives.

The average human being prefers to be directed, wishes to avoid responsibility, has relatively little ambition, wants security above all.

McGregor's Theory X was not intended to define people as they are, but as he felt many managers tended to view them. Manuals of policies and procedures in many organizations fairly scream the message, "If you don't watch them every minute, they'll take advantage of you." *They,* of course, are the employees upon whom you must depend. The manuals deal with every kind of problem and contingency—how much time off is permitted for this and that, what to do in the case of infraction of the 1000 rules, how to discipline.

Some policy manuals should bear the title *The Organizational Playground.* In reading them, one has the picture of teachers and monitors standing about watching for the slightest violation of rules by the children. And, in fact, many organizations seem not to know how to treat employees as adults.

How managers compensate

FEAR

When motivation and commitment by employees to organizational objectives are low, managers try to find ways to compensate. Overcontrolling employees is one such form of compensation. It is, if anything, an endorsement of Theory X. It can also be regarded as a statement of helplessness: We don't know how employees can be motivated to do a good job, so we use fear. There is fear of being embarrassed by one's boss before one's peers. There is fear of punishment. There is fear of losing one's job.

Fear is a widely used substitute for motivation management. What's the payoff for doing a good job? "We let you keep it," replies the fear manager. It's a big joke, of course. Everyone laughs. And they should, because fear is a poor motivator. True, the employee may see value in avoiding punishment, but avoidance as a motivating force operates strongly for only a short time. After a while, even in an economy that most of us have accepted as cyclical, many employees would have no compunction in telling this vestige of the Depression era *where* he could stow his job.

MANIPULATION

Another compensating device for poor motivation techniques is manipulation. That term as I use it always implies deception. The rationale for manipulation is usually that employees can't or won't be turned on to something for the real reason, so management must substitute a goal that is phony or at least withhold the real reason for the job. For example, one manager was urged to move from one division of a company to another. The vice-president, two management levels above her, explained that the new position would give her a greater chance to use her special mix of talents. It was an opportunity that cried out for her. The fact was that the move was being suggested not because of her ability but because the manager's boss had quietly complained to the vice-president about his inability to work with her. She knew something of the complaining, and a great deal of the incompatibility. Top management saw the move as the way to correct a serious problem, while pretending that there was no problem. The young manager viewed the explanation as manipulation, pure deception. She said it would have been more acceptable to her if the move had been described to her for what it was—a solution to a sticky problem.

Sometimes a manager will be reluctant to assign a particular job, foreseeing that an employee may hesitate to accept it. So, as an inducement, the manager will paint the job as something it is not. For example, a young branch manager was persuaded to take on an assignment in another part of the country because it offered a challenge. No one else wanted it because one of the largest distributors in the area was known to be a son of a gun to work with. The young branch manager was told, "Look, if you can pull this off, you can write your own ticket in the company."

The branch manager did the first—he built a rapport and a very profitable relationship with the difficult distributor. He tried to do the second—write his own ticket. He found that no one had taken the promise seriously, or indeed, even knew what it meant. Ironically, the truth would have been sufficient: He was being offered a challenging assignment that few could have handled. The knowledge that he was one of the few would have been ample reward.

Manipulation is a game. It is seduction. Sometimes it is an out-and-out lie. And when it becomes exposed as that, it loses its power because trust in the manager is essential to motivation. If you, the manager, tell me, the employee, that if I do this, such-and-such will follow, then, barring circumstances that no one could have foreseen, that result had better follow. If it doesn't, and I suspect you had no interest in fulfilling the contract, then you lose credibility with me. Manipulation is a desperate, shortsighted approach to persuading employees to do what you want them to do without telling them why you really want them to do it. It stops working long before the manipulator is aware of it. Employees will have long since begun to play their own games, one of which is, how-can-we-make-the-boss-think-he-is-still-getting-his-way?

I am suspicious of any manager who, in talking of a subordinate, says, "Here's how you handle him." It usually suggests manipulation of the person. It also suggests a self-delusion on the part of the manager. I would wager that the employee has already become aware of the manager's "handling" tactics.

BEING NICE TO PEOPLE

There are other ways managers try to compensate for uncertain or poor motivation management. One flows from the human relations school. The basic tenet of this approach to management: If you are nice to employees, they will be happy and work better. Experience has not established this as a workable premise. Generally employees are there to achieve certain things they want—money, status, and other rewards and reinforcements that we shall cover in depth later. If you help them achieve these objectives, the probabilities are that they will work better. Your being nice, patient, considerate, a careful listener, maintaining an open door policy, expressing interest in their personal problems, putting their welfare above all other considerations, may add a pleasant frosting. These things will not, however, take the place of effective management that gets results— for everyone.

There simply are not convincing data to support the approach of the human relations school. All that we really know about happy employees is that they are happy employees. Happy employees do not necessarily produce better than unhappy employees, although it is undoubtedly true that most people, employees and managers alike, would prefer to work in an environment that is pleasant and warmly human.

Paternalism is an old and familiar approach to hooking employees. It is a variant of the human relations approach. The paternalistic manager emphasizes loyalty to management and the organization. Management is a benevolent master, giving lots of benefits, being very considerate up to a point of the employee as a whole person. But no one is ever permitted to forget the master part. Fathers provide a nice place to work and take good care of their employees. But paternalism is often spoken of scornfully these days by employees who can read the purpose of the niceness. It is a means by which management gets what it wants, without genuine concern for the objectives of the employees. As one employee of a large organization put it, "That's how they buy us."

A concern for morale is often indicative of the people-should-be-happy approach. Morale is often used in connection with motivation, and I am by no means sure of their relationship to each another. I have worked in situations in which the productivity of employees was exceptionally high even though the morale was abysmally low. I happen to believe that, over a prolonged period, morale does have a relationship to productivity. That is, sustained high productivity requires high morale. But that belief remains unproven by scientific data, and the role of job satisfaction continues to be the subject of an intense and continuing debate. Asking people how they feel about what they are doing produces a lot of interesting information, but what to do with it is still open to question.

The influence of style

This chapter would not be complete without an evaluation of management style and its effects on motivation. It is probably safe to say that every manager has his or her own favorite approach to dealing with subordinates. Some managers are said to be very task oriented. The phrase means that the task comes first. The manager's relationships with employees are of lesser concern. But the tasks get done. And employees who are interested in the rewards that achieving those tasks can bring often get highly turned on in this environment. The world of the arts, especially, provides a long list of artistic directors who were tyrants yet who inspired outstanding performances from others and intense loyalty.

It used to be fashionable to make a distinction between the task-oriented manager and the people-oriented one. This distinction is simplistic. It is more realistic to say that a manager needs people to get the tasks done, and a manager who is truly concerned with people realizes that they need tasks to accomplish. From that perspective, whether a manager starts with the task or the people, the result should be the same.

Probably the chief difficulty of a style—any style—is that it does not work equally well with all employees. No across-the-board approach will.

There are at least three questions a manager must ask about style: Am I comfortable with it because it reflects me, how I feel about the job, the people who report to me, the organization itself? (You'd better not be too much out of step with the rest of the organization or people get uncomfortable.) Does it facilitate the work so that we can meet goals? Does it help the employees to do what they are capable of doing and what they want to do?

If the answers to these questions are yes, then it is likely the manager has hit upon the right combination for him or her. It will work some of the time with some of the people. But there is still the matter of how to deal with the people individually and in different situations when a particular style isn't effective. Style implies a fairly consistent approach to people—an approach that is indeed reflective of you, that seems to fit you comfortably, will at least help to build people's trust. People will know what to expect of you.

The more difficult and complex question is how you can know what to expect from each of your subordinates. And how you can translate those expectations into significant goals that people value. The first step in that translation is understanding some of the significant findings of research in motivation theory.

3. Important beginnings in motivation theory

It was an exciting day in 1966 when a colleague at the Research Institute brought a newly published book into an editorial meeting and began to quote from it. The book was *Work and the Nature of Man* and the author was Frederick Herzberg, a behavioral scientist then at Case-Western Reserve University. Herzberg seemed to be saying new things about people at work. For example, salary is not a motivator. It had been traditional for managers to believe that the prime motivator for most people was money. Yet, here was a suggestion that there are other aspects of work that turned them on more than money—the work itself, responsibility, achievement. Herzberg's work challenged the traditional views of people so well defined by McGregor's Theory X.

In fact, some of the things Herzberg said had already been pointed to by Douglas McGregor and psychologist Abraham Maslow, to cite just two. Herzberg's new book seemed to add impetus. From that time on, no speaker or writer on management issues could afford to ignore the trio. It didn't seem to make any difference what specific point the author or speaker was addressing, reference had to be made to Maslow, Herzberg, and McGregor. Yet, the real significance of the theories—as well as their limitations—was often overlooked.

Maslow's hierarchy of needs

The first of the trio to become well known was Abraham H. Maslow, professor of psychology at Brandeis University and president of the American Psychological Association. His book, *Motivation and Personality*, published in 1954, defined what became Maslow's trademark, a "Hierarchy of Needs."

People are motivated, according to Maslow, to satisfy certain needs ranging from the very basic and bodily to the very complex and psychological. Here are the needs in ascending order of complexity:

Physiological: Bodily needs such as food, sex, drink, sleep;

Safety: The desire to be secure, to have stability, protection, freedom from fear; the need for structure and order;

Belongingness and Love: The wish to have friends, family, contact, intimacy;

Esteem: The desire to have the esteem of others as well as to feel self-esteem, to be competent and be regarded as useful, important;

Self-Actualization: To grow, to become what one is capable of being, a process in which one's potential is realized.

Maslow says that a person feels a particular higher need only when the needs lower in the hierarchy are *predominantly* satisfied. A need that has been largely satisfied does not motivate. Thus, a person has little drive for security or love when the stomach is crying for food.

But when is a need predominantly satisfied? That's an essential question, and the answer has never been clear. Take the very lowest—physiological. Is that need satisfied when the appetite is sated, or when there is assurance that the need can be met with ease? Does the need become a motivator when, say, hunger asserts itself? Or does it cease to motivate when a ready supply of food exists?

As one ascends the hierarchy, the issues become more complex. One may make love or seek physical intimacy not only for sexual release (physiological needs) but also to achieve feelings of power over another—or even to win the esteem of others who may see the act as one of conquest.

Maslow suggests that a need may have been satisfied for such a long time that it has become undervalued, its motivational force reduced. One may enjoy such wide esteem of others for so long that it doesn't any longer seem important. That being the case, the esteemed person may actually feel a more intense need for love from one person, which is lower in the hierarchy.

A NEW LOOK AT PEOPLE

The hierarchy seemed so simple when it first appeared. That was probably one key to its tremendous appeal. Another was undoubtedly its positive view of people at work, again a challenge to the traditional portrayal of the unwilling worker.

Only later did people realize that the hierarchy raises many more questions than it answers. Furthermore, it is sometimes very difficult to translate general needs into specific objectives. If we are to understand what motivates people and utilize that understanding in management, then we must know what objectives they are working to attain at a given time. For example, it is not enough to say that Gerald Murphy works hard as a supervisor because he seeks the esteem of other supervisors and higher management. Is he always motivated by esteem? Undoubtedly there are times when Murphy is working to satisfy other needs. But how can Murphy's boss know? The problem is that the hierarchy may explain a general *why* of employee behavior without showing the manager what can be done to influence it specifically.

What undoubtedly was most important about Maslow at the time was the recognition that people—individual human beings—have needs they strive to fill, that those needs are complex, and that the needs a person is trying to satisfy today may be quite different from tomorrow or next week. Needs in people vary from day to day, task to task, situation to situation. The hierarchy pointed to those variables without, of course, suggesting how managers might deal with them. The implications for anyone who supervised the work of others were clearly enormous.

That employees have needs higher than those of mere hunger and security was suggested by the Hawthorne Studies of the late 1920s and early 1930s, at a Western Electric plant. A team headed by Harvard's Elton Mayo had developed evidence that employees responded productively to more considerate supervision and control over their work. But the Depression halted the Hawthorne research, and it was two decades before Maslow's refinements of the Hawthorne analysis achieved wide attention.

SELF-ACTUALIZATION

One significant advancement of Maslow was his concept of self-actualization, which is the process of achieving one's potential, of becoming what one is capable of being. This need is quite different from the lower needs. If people don't have enough food or esteem or love, they work to acquire them. They don't have a choice. These are so-called deficit needs, demanding to be filled. But Maslow saw people who seek to actualize themselves, doing so not out of a deficiency but to initiate a stage in their growth. Some people never really reach this stage; hence, they are never impelled to begin the process of self-actualization.

People at the self-actualizing level of development work for material rewards, but for many other kinds as well—pride, satisfaction in doing a good job, a sense of accomplishment, a desire to grow, to develop skills and talents. They are especially alert to what is going on around them. They frequently see new things—or old things in a fresh way. They are creative and problem-centered rather than self-centered.

However, the need to self-actualize is bound to cause problems for most people in most organizations, where the autonomy of the self-actualizer is difficult to achieve and where the opportunities to develop—to actualize— so many talents are severely limited. Perhaps it is realistic to say that a person in organizational life is more often actualized according to the needs of the organization than to his or her own.

However many are the gaps left unfilled and questions unanswered by the hierarchy, there is no question that the humanism of Abraham Maslow began to break down barriers and molds. The better-educated, newly affluent working population of the 1950s and early 1960s was beginning to discard the old perception of people as economic animals, working only for subsistence and material gain. Many of these people thought in terms of careers, not just jobs. In the era of the so-called Organization Man, it was refreshing to believe that people worked to satisfy needs that were on a plane higher than the paycheck. People recognized that they received rewards from doing the work itself, feelings of achievement and satisfaction that came from within.

McGregor's Theory Y

Douglas McGregor, whose Theory X we have already looked at in the previous chapter, was heavily influenced by the direction of Maslow's thinking. A professor at M.I.T. and former president of Antioch College, McGregor wanted to formulate what he regarded as a more contemporary way of looking at people at work. The traditional view was expressed by Theory X. The more modern assumptions are described in Theory Y:

The expenditure of physical and mental effort in work is as natural as in play or rest.

External control and the threat of punishment are not the only means for bringing about effort toward organizational objectives. One will exercise self-direction and self-control in the service of objectives to which he or she is committed.

Commitment to objectives is a function of the rewards associated with achievement of those objectives.

The average human being learns, under proper conditions, not merely to accept but to seek responsibility.

The capacity to exercise a relatively high degree of imagination, ingenuity, and creativity in the solution of organizational problems is widely, not narrowly, distributed in the population.

Under the conditions of modern industrial life, the intellectual potentialities of the average human being are only partially utilized.

Theory Y sees people working because it is natural. People work not to avoid something—punishment or starvation, for example—but to achieve something that is valuable to them. They don't need to be dependent upon and controlled by others in all that they do; they actually seek responsibility so as to have some control over their own efforts (a theme that has become increasingly important in the behavioral sciences and work). The effective organization does not so much create controls and penalties as remove the obstacles to better performance by the people who are part of the organization.

Maslow theorized that people have material, psychological, and social needs, and that they seek to satisfy them. McGregor took the theory further and said that people will work to satisfy those needs *in a job.* It takes only a short jump to assume that people can identify with the goals of the organization if through achieving those goals they can fill their own needs.

McGregor caught on with many managers, probably because they felt that Theory Y assumptions described *them*, though not necessarily their subordinates. The appeal of McGregor was also undoubtedly due to the easily definable categories of X and Y.

TWO KINDS OF MANAGEMENT?

Thus, during the 1960s it became commonplace—though not accurate—to speak of Theory X or Theory Y management. If managers tended to be autocratic, controlling, tough, task-oriented; if they declined to trust employees to work on their own without constant, skeptical supervision; if they took it for granted people would cheat, lie, take shortcuts rather than put out a fair day's work; then they were labeled Theory X managers. The leadership style reflecting any of the above was termed Theory X management.

Theory Y management in contrast was open and trusting, democratic as opposed to autocratic, concerned with people, extending authority and responsibility further down in the organization, involving employees in decisions that affected them and their work. Human relations became a familiar, honored term.

In the late 1960s, a colleague observed that managers she knew seemed to look at themselves, their peers, and their bosses through Theory Y glasses, while still making Theory X assumptions about subordinates. I suspect there was truth to that. Ironically, these days managers often ask me, "What do you do with a Theory X boss?" The implication is that the manager feels that he or she understands the Theory Y nature of subordinates—but his or her own boss does not.

What many managers forgot was that McGregor was not attempting to give a definitive description of people, their motivations, their attitudes toward work. He certainly was not saying that there are two kinds of people—or two ways of looking at them. To McGregor,

X and Y were only two points on a continuum. Nor was he under any illusion that he was producing the ultimate management manual (which many assumed would be based on Theory Y).

The managers forgot because it is always so tempting to see people as members of groups, to apply labels indiscriminately. Exchanging one set of assumptions about humanity for another doesn't necessarily result in going from an ineffective management style to an effective one; in fact, it often perpetuates a hit-or-miss tradition of managing people. There are, in any organization, some people who want more direction and some who want less. There are employees who take pleasure in being creative and innovative; there are those who feel no need or inclination to be so. Some people derive their greatest satisfactions from activities off the job, regarding work as the way of subsidizing those outside interests. Some human beings are psychologically dependent upon others; others are autonomous and prefer to direct themselves.

The primary importance of Theory Y is that McGregor made it respectable to think in terms of people achieving personal objectives through their efforts to help organizations achieve *their* objectives. It was a small but highly significant jump to the suggestion that the kind of work people did could be important to them, that the work itself could be a powerful motivator.

Herzberg's two-factor theory

It was Frederick Herzberg, mentioned earlier in the chapter, who sought to show through research that people could be motivated by the work itself, that accomplishing organizational tasks and objectives could fulfill a human need, and that job content could be varied to serve as a greater or a lesser motivating force, depending partly on its degree of challenge.

Herzberg, now at the University of Utah, developed

the two-factor theory, the components of which are job satisfiers and dissatisfiers. First advanced in the 1959 book *The Motivation to Work,* and fleshed out in *Work and the Nature of Man,* published in 1966, the theory describes job satisfiers or motivators. The following are considered by Herzberg to be motivators:

Achievement: The successful completion of a job or task; a solution; the results of one's work;

Recognition of achievement: An act of praise or some other notice of the achievement;

Work itself: Tasks as sources of good feelings about the work done; extent of duties;

Responsibility: For one's own work or that of others; new tasks and assignments;

Advancement: An actual improvement in status or position;

Possibility for growth: Potential to rise in the organization.

These are the factors that motivate and satisfy people, that encourage them to want to work—and to work well. The presence of any of these factors will satisfy or motivate; however, their absence will not necessarily demotivate or cause dissatisfaction.

According to Herzberg, there is another set of influences on how an employee views the job: dissatisfiers (also called hygiene or maintenance factors). While they don't motivate, and their presence won't provide job satisfaction, their absence will create dissatisfaction:

Supervision: Willingness or unwillingness to teach or to delegate responsibility that can result in things running smoothly or being irritating;

Company policy and administration: Structure, good or bad communications, adequate or inadequate authority, harmful or beneficial effects of company and personnel policies;

Positive working conditions: Environmental and physical conditions;

Interpersonal relations with peers, subordinates, and superiors: The social and working transactions with others on the job;

Status: How one's position or standing is perceived by others; perquisites of rank;

Job security: Stability, tenure;

Salary: Compensation;

Personal life: How aspects of the work—such as long hours or required transfer and relocation—affect the employee's personal life.

Herzberg's research threatened to poke more holes in an already ragged popular belief. People are not necessarily motivated by bright, cheery, well-lighted work places. A pleasant supervisor does not automatically provide a reason to work harder. Despite a long-prevailing view, it seems that people are not driven to attain job security.

Salary, not a motivator as such, can play an important role as a symbol of recognition of achievement, for, in Herzberg's terms, such recognition *is* a motivator. Also, salary can be linked so closely with growth and advancement that it may be difficult to decide if it is a satisfier or a dissatisfier. The varied roles of money in motivation have not been thoroughly studied. It may be that dollars have a direct short-term, rather than long-term, influence. For example, the person who is led to believe in October that a special effort will result in a large raise in January could conceivably be motivated to work hard to get the extra money. However, once the raise has been granted, the money is no longer a motivator.

Money is not the only ambiguity in the theory. Surroundings may not motivate, but the prospect of a large, cheery, corner office may—as recognition of achievement. Supervision does not act as a motivator, but a supervisor can provide motivating factors: growth opportunities and increased responsibilities.

Nevertheless, the two-factor theory confirmed the trend in motivation thinking: People *can* satisfy needs through work and through helping organizations to achieve their needs, even though those needs may be hard to recognize.

The popularity of this trio of writers was probably due to several factors. First, partly as a function of affluence and education, we were open to a more humane view of people at work. Most people, it is safe to say, saw in themselves the higher, achieving, creative needs suggested by the new theories. The research was, well, flattering. Too, the new body of work presented some convenient, easy-to-use labels. No doubt, many people could not resist the temptation to apply them.

But what is most important is that the time for the ideas had come. People were ready to accept them. After that, what was needed was a new technology. The new thinking sounded good, and it read well. But much more help was needed—specific pragmatic help. How could managers use this thinking? How could they derive practical techniques to increase the effectiveness of people on the job?

The work of two other psychologists provided some further answers—and brought managers closer to that technology.

4: Why people do as they do

People have needs, says Maslow. Those needs are expressed at work, which is very important to people, say McGregor and Herzberg. Needs can be translated into goals.

But it isn't enough to set goals and watch people head for them. It isn't just a matter of winding employees up, pointing them in the direction you want them to take, and then letting them go. That is a lesson many supporters of "Management By Objectives" have learned to their chagrin. In the early days of MBO, many managers assumed that all you had to do was explain what you wanted done and why: If people could see how the part they play fits into the function and purpose of the whole organization, they would be motivated. It's not that simple. People make choices between goals that are important to *them.*

Why they make certain choices—and *how* the manager can influence those choices—is explained more specifically by two similar theories. One is the development of Victor Vroom of Yale. The other is the Social Learning Theory as advanced by Julian Rotter of the University of Connecticut. Surprisingly, neither name is well known among managers today.

Both theories hold that people make choices between this course of action and that. The boss announces that he wants everyone to clear up all of the customer correspondence by quitting time. The employees ask themselves, "Do I put on the extra steam required, or do I work at my usual pace and let him worry about it?"

There are innumerable other choices employees ponder: "I've been offered the Des Moines branch. Do I take it or wait for a branch in California to open up?"

"The assistant controller's job will be coming up soon. But it will involve supervising the work of other people. Should I take on the responsibility of others or continue to do my thing?"

"It's a beautiful afternoon and only 3:30. Should I try to squeeze two more sales calls in or knock off now?"

These choices have much to do with whether I take on this job or that, perform this function or assignment as opposed to another, do my work well or just adequately (or not at all), go after a goal that is my manager's or one that is my own, concentrate on job-related goals or put most of my energy into my off-the-job interests.

It is obvious that managers need to be concerned very much with the choices—both everyday and long-range—that employees make. Those choices reflect the motivating forces within those people. If managers ignore the import of those choices, management becomes a haphazard affair. If, on the other hand, they learn how to understand the choosing process and how the process can be influenced, then managers can see the way to greater effectiveness.

According to the thinking of Vroom and Rotter, there are these principal factors in the choices people make:

1 *The value of the goal.* What will be the result of my doing this as opposed to that? How much more valuable to me is choice A than Choice B? I realize that it is important to the boss that all of the correspondence be finished by five o'clock; but if that achievement is not sufficiently important to me, I'll continue to work at my usual speed even if it means not getting finished.

2 *Probability of succeeding.* It isn't enough for the

results of my choice or action to be valuable to me. I must also believe that I have a reasonable chance to achieve those results. I would like a promotion, but I don't think I have managerial ability. I would probably fail as assistant controller.

3 *The situation.* Rotter believes that the situation influences my choice or my behavior. I may, for example, like to be known as a raconteur. But if my stock of stories is largely risqué, I may forego the role when invited to dinner at the company president's house. There's no question that environment, location, conditions under which a job is to be done can influence a choice of behavior.

These are factors that influence a person's behavior, and many times a manager can affect the force of those factors. For example, the manager can do so by building more value into a job, by making the employee's anticipation of success more confident, and by adjusting the conditions under which the job will be done.

The remainder of the book will demonstrate how you can influence all three factors—value, probability, and situation—to enhance the motivation, hence the productivity of employees.

Value

People choose to do what they consider valuable to them, as I've stated. They work to achieve or gain something that they perceive as good for them. They will not choose a goal that they expect to be harmful to them.

Many managers get hung up on this point. What an employee will choose to do, how the employee behaves, is mysterious to them. They can't empathize or sympathize. "Can't John see how his argumentative personality offends the boss?" one such manager might ask about a co-worker. Perhaps John doesn't see how his arguing upsets his boss. Instead, he believes that he is influencing the boss. Or perhaps John values himself as a winner of arguments, which is why he works so hard at it. It's a matter of competitiveness. Still another possibility is that the goal John wants most is annoying the fellow he has to report to. I've only begun to explore all of the possibilities. One thing is certain: John doesn't see that his actions hurt him, although others may. Somehow he feels rewarded in what he does.

Sometimes people seek punishment. One woman told me of a co-worker who periodically became intoxicated, and either showed up at her door or telephoned her. She sternly lectured her drunken friend each time. She scolded and admonished her. The more often the friend showed up, the more harsh the critic became. But instead of avoiding her critical friend, the heavy drinker sought her out more frequently—behavior that was a mystery to the young woman. What she didn't understand was that the friend felt guilty and wanted to be told just how weak and disgusting she was.

FIND THE REWARD

When managers describe subordinates' behavior that puzzles them, my response is usually, "Look for the rewards." The subordinates feel that they have good reasons. That's a distinction that too often eludes managers. Many people project their values onto others. "Can't she see what a great opportunity this could be for her?" What a person is saying in such a statement is how much he or she would value a similar opportunity.

Managers would find much of the behavior that puzzles them to be more reasonable if, instead of shaking their heads, they stopped to ask themselves, "Where is the reward for the person who is doing that?" The reason for the behavior is not always readily apparent, but you can be certain that it is there. Furthermore, the reason has appeal to the person doing the act even if it does not to you.

Managers cripple their effectiveness when they assume that subordinates share their own values. A young engineer with an M.B.A. degree was transferred from an upstate New York division of a large organization to the New York headquarters. There he was assigned to a department that prepared bids for engineering work. Once he learned how to evaluate cost and to construct a bid, he found the work boring. In a conversation with his boss one day at lunch, he confided that he was restless. His boss stiffened and said, "I don't know why. I've been doing this work for twelve years and I've never had a boring day."

Obviously the manager's feelings about the job didn't match those of the subordinate. And the manager simply assumed the subordinate should feel the way he did. Communications hardly got better. The young M.B.A. left for more challenge elsewhere.

Challenge, incidentally, is one kind of reward or motivational factor. It is closely related to achievement, advancement, and growth—motivators that Herzberg has identified. It is a good example of an internal reward or reinforcer. Challenge is only one of many kinds of rewards we'll consider in this book. Remember, though, that when behavior is rewarded it is reinforced. Reinforcement encourages repetition of that behavior. That's something all of us learned (or most of us, anyway) in school: Hard work usually brought good grades, which encouraged more hard work.

The grades were *external* reinforcers or rewards, granted by others. Internal rewards are those that we generate ourselves as a result of having achieved something—for example, a sense of satisfaction about the new knowledge we gained after studying so hard.

Probability

Probability of success in a job or on a task is another area in which managers project their own feelings. A manager assigns a goal, comfortable in the assurance that achieving it would pose no great problem. But that is the manager's perception of the employee's chances of successful attainment. Small wonder that, when the employee balks or even fails at the task, the manager is baffled or annoyed.

There has to be, *in the employee's mind,* a reasonable chance of achieving the goal. If the reward is very attractive, the employee will probably commit himself or herself to the task. That may be true also when the value of the goal is moderate but the chance of doing the job well is great. Some people will go for that kind of a goal. But even though the reward is great, if the chance of success is slim, most people will shy away. A young woman looking for an upwardly mobile career is told that computer technology is one good bet. But she knows she is terrible at mathematics. It's not likely that she'll look for opportunities in computers.

Once again, as in determining the value of a goal, managers must meet employees where they are—not where the managers are themselves. Probability of success, of achievement, or *expectation,* is in the performer's mind. That's where it counts. How the observer views the performer's probability of achievement may or may not resemble the latter's expectancy.

There may be any number of reasons why an employee may have low expectations about being able to complete a task or job, or pursue a particular career. He or she may be thinking, "I don't know enough"; "there's not enough time"; "I don't have enough equipment or the right kind of people"; "my health won't stand up"— or any one of a number of other obstacles.

Managers sometimes make serious mistakes when they assume they understand how employees feel about their abilities to function. Or when they assume that employees will admit their low expectations to their managers. The reluctance to tell all, that is, to say, "I don't want to take this work on because I don't think I can do it, and here's why" is understandable when *why* means risking failure now and a lack of advancement later, loss of face, erosion of self-confidence, or other blows to the ego or to the career. It's usually easier to find out how much value employees attach to goals than to get a fix on how they see their ability to do it.

Situation

The third factor affecting an employee's on-the-job commitment is the situation in which work will be done—the circumstances or conditions surrounding it. Keep in mind that behavior doesn't take place in a vacuum. The circumstances help to determine whether a certain kind of behavior is desired, or appropriate, or useful. Julian Rotter points to the example of the small boy who, alone with his mother, wants her kisses. But when playing with his boyfriends, he resists her efforts to show affection. Clearly, the one reward, his mother's kisses, is subordinate to the desired esteem of his friends. The value of the first goal is changed because of the change in situation.

A manager must not make the error of assigning work in a vacuum. For example, a manager is considering a particular task. The manager knows that it has to be valuable to the employee. Let's assume that the employee is confident of doing it well. The manager does not envision any other obstacle: "Here's the chance you've been waiting for—to show what you have in a highly visible job. Our Phoenix office is in trouble. Go out there and give them a hand. If you pull this off, there's no doubt you'll get your own regional office."

But the troubleshooter soon realizes that the Phoenix office is in very bad shape. It may take several months to turn around. Perhaps it will never be turned around. The people in Phoenix have indicated that they don't think that this fellow from New York can teach them anything. There's no question about the value of the assignment—a regional office is waiting down the road. And even though these people in Phoenix are hard nuts, the challenge is great and exciting. Perhaps success could lead to a vice-presidency.

However, there is another factor. The assignment will mean much time away from home. Ordinarily that might not be a problem. But the engineer's wife is pregnant and is not carrying the child well. He considers the situation and decides this is a poor time to be away for an extended period. Yes, the reward would be important, but it has, for the moment, lost its value. The job, though difficult, can be done. Still, the responsibility of caring for his wife, has taken precedence.

Thus the situation surrounding the work—the environment, location, people involved, personal circumstances—may diminish the value or the expectancy of success. What works or may be desirable in one situation, under one set of conditions, may not in another. Complicated? Very. But all three of these factors are considered by employees when weighing choices or making commitments to the work, to the manager's or organization's objectives. It almost goes without saying that managers have also to take these factors into consideration if they want those commitments from subordinates.

5: The importance of goals

Aside from the fact that goals determine behavior, on-the-job goals or objectives (I use the words interchangeably) fulfill a number of needs:

They give order and structure. Remember that Maslow defined these as *safety* needs, just above food, drink, sleep, and sex. We all require some order and structure in our lives.

They measure progress. Most of us have the need to be going somewhere. We aren't happy to mark time. When we recognize and work toward goals, we have a sense of movement. We can see the direction we are moving and the pace.

They give a sense of achievement. Frederick Herzberg identifies achievement as a motivator. People take pride in their accomplishment. Closely allied with achievement is the fact that goals . . .

Provide closure. Most people like something that has limits, that comes to an end. Too many open-ended activities can frustrate, leave the feeling that one is not really getting anywhere.

They create feedback and information for the manager. You need to know where people are investing their time and energies, how well they are investing them. A goal is one kind of control that you need to monitor and adjust performance.

Why some goal setting doesn't work

If goals are natural and so helpful to managers and subordinates alike, why do so many organizations report having so many problems with management-by-objectives? MBO is an approach to achieve periodic goal setting at the many levels of an organization. The overall objectives of the organization are reflected up and down the line. In theory MBO seems to be a natural; people should take to it as they take to walking or talking. But many MBO programs have failed or have produced disappointing results.

Having goals is natural, of course. But the process of thinking them through and setting them is learned. Most of the reasons we have for doing what we do are not being identified and thought through each time. Many of them have become ritualized. We behave in certain ways for reasons that may have been established long ago.

On the job, people are asked to sit down on a regular basis to examine what needs to be accomplished and to set priorities (some goals are more important than others). Those people—managers and subordinates—need to be trained to do it. Often they are not.

Goals should not be confused with quotas. The latter are usually imposed. The individual who is responsible for filling the quota may or may not have enthusiasm for doing so. He or she may not even care very much whether it is filled.

In the early days of MBO, many managers worked with quotas rather than set goals. To use a simple illustration, managers at the top of the organization established a goal of twenty thousand units (of whatever) for the coming year. At each level of the hierarchy the total number of units was carved up, with each manager accepting a piece of the action. Managers would sit down with subordinates and say something such as, "We have to turn out five hundred units. Now, how can we do this?"

That was the process that many managers believed was MBO. It was based on two incomplete managerial axioms: The first was, "Don't just tell them, tell them why"; and the second, "Show employees how what they do fits in with the overall structure." Both axioms are commendable, so far as they go. But, as I'll discuss, people need to assume some responsibility for setting goals. When goals are imposed, people often don't feel committed to them.

There are other reasons why goal-setting approaches often fail. Here are eight that I have isolated:

1 *Too many.* Either no attempt is made to identify the priority of goals or they are listed in order of priority —all of them. There are just so many goals that people can attend to. It's probably safe to say that many goals, involving familiar activities or extensions of tasks that are performed regularly, do not have to be restated as goals each time. When something becomes too familiar, it usually becomes unexciting.

2 *Insufficient accountability.* Goals are set but not always followed up. Let's say that five goals are established for a given period. At the end of that period, progress toward all five, not just some of them, must be measured. Goals that get lost between the cracks suggest that the manager wasn't all that serious to begin with. And the employee wonders if the manager wasn't really concerned about that one, maybe he or she isn't serious about some of the others either. Conclusion: don't set goals unless you're prepared to follow through on them.

3 *Too much forgiveness.* In this case, all goals are followed up, but if managers do not meet objectives, they are forgiven. This has the effect of negating the importance of the goals. If objectives are not met, the reasons should be explored. Perhaps the goals were not realistic, or the performance was inadequate, or there

were external factors that created barriers—or all three. Once the reasons are accepted, then adjustments have to be made. But simply dismissing the failure to meet objectives will serve to diminish their importance. "Don't worry about it" will soon become the prevailing attitude.

4 *Too few subgoals.* The overall objectives may be set for long-term periods. If you rely solely upon the goals as defined, you won't know how well you are progressing toward them until you near the end of the time period. You need to measure progress as you go. You may have to make adjustments in the goal or the performance mid-period. Furthermore, achieving subgoals gives employees a sense of progress that encourages them to completion.

5 *Conflicting priorities.* Sometimes managers will impose priorities that are important to them. For example, the manager decides that what matters is that all employees be at their desks promptly at 8:30. This becomes a paramount consideration, taking precedence over performance goals that employees accept as more meaningful. Employees may never wholly accept the manager's priorities, especially if they are imposed or seem illogical.

6 *Ego goals.* The manager starts a project that employees don't regard as useful or possible. In one department, a superior mused, "Maybe we ought to think about . . ." and it was enough to prompt the department head to take the bare threads proposed by his boss and try to put together a suit. Employees saw many of these plans and projects more as schemes for the manager's own glorification than as worthwhile investments of energy and time. To the employees they were distractions, even barriers to effectiveness.

7 *Managerial lack of interest.* The manager who sets goals for and with employees, then shows little or no interest, provides no real support, is courting employees' lack of interest. Managers have to achieve a balance between giving employees total independence to achieve goals their own way and directing them every step of the way. Once a goal is set, the manager is well advised to show interest and concern. Otherwise the message is broadcast that the manager doesn't really care.

8 *Withholding managerial resources.* If you have the time, knowledge, experience, or skill that would enhance the success of employees in achieving objectives, let everyone know that you are available to them as a resource. Otherwise employees may feel rather exposed on the firing line, and their resentment over that exposure and their hesitation to take undue risks by themselves may get in the way of accomplishing the organizational objectives.

Conveying expectations

There was a famous experiment involving school children in San Francisco that demonstrated that expectations of performance can have an effect on the performance itself. In the experiment, some teachers were to give assignments and express their expectations that the students would do them well. Other teachers, giving assignments, would express lower expectations or would be noncommittal. Teachers who expressed their belief that the students would do a good job achieved better performances from students than teachers who expressed lesser or no expectations.

There is a clear message for managers in these results: You can have a positive effect on performance by letting people know that you expect them to perform according to your standards. Goals are an expression of what you expect from the people who work for you. "We agree, then, that by the end of the next quarter, your staff will be able to classify the leads from our advertising campaign by sales district, and within the district by size of company, type of business, and product interest, and send out 80 percent of the leads to salespeople within seventy-two hours of receipt. That allows for an extra heavy load of leads, people out sick or on vacation, or some unexpected condition." There's an objective that clearly states what is to be accomplished by what time. It clearly conveys standards.

Managers too often take it for granted that employees know what the managers expect them to do— what is to be done, what is an acceptable standard, by whom and when. I've had managers say, "Well, the work is right in front of them. For example, if they're stocking shelves, and the shelves are empty, they know they're supposed to get the merchandise and put it up." I am not trying to be contentious for the sake of contention, but look at the inadequacy of that. At what point does the stocker replenish the shelves? Half empty? A quarter empty? What happens to older merchandise? Does it need to be pushed to the front? Are there occasional other duties, such as working on a cash register when the store is crowded, that may take precedence over stocking shelves?

Or managers will say, "There's a position description for the job. It tells them what their duties are." Position descriptions usually don't convey standards or priorities. People need to know them to do a good job.

I repeat: Goals are an effective way for you to express to subordinates what you expect of them. Goals tell them how their performance will be evaluated, and on what basis they will be rewarded.

The three Rs of goals

Goals that work in motivation display at least these three characteristics:

1 *Realistic.* If they are, it means that people can achieve them. A goal that is too low offers no challenge, little interest. Goals that are too routine, extensions of

what the employee does now or knows how to do quite competently, invite a ho-hum response. A goal that is too high offers a great deal of risk, perhaps little chance of attainment, which can lead to frustration. When the employee comes to believe that the goal is out of reach, he or she may give up.

Goals may need to be adjusted upward or downward. That's one value of setting subgoals. If they're too easily accomplished, then the goal will lose its challenge. It needs to be raised. But if the subgoal is seriously missed, and if the employee is showing frustration, then the goal can be adjusted downward a bit for the next time period. If you don't step in to adjust an improbably high goal, de-motivation will usually occur.

2 *Relevant to the organization.* It helps to be able to show that a particular goal makes a contribution to the organization's success and well-being. That way employees can relate their efforts to those of others, and they can take legitimate credit in their achievement and that of the organization as a whole. (Interestingly, early MBO efforts often concentrated on this R, and failed because the other two Rs were neglected.)

3 *Relate to the person.* Why is this goal important to the individual employee? The subordinate knows what the organization will get from the goal; what will the employee gain from working to achieve it? Of course, you can reward that achievement, and it's vital that employees know that their successful efforts will be recognized. But it's time also to consider what you know of the employee, what the person regards as valuable, some of the information that the following chapter encourages you to collect.

Four kinds of goals

Some goals originate up the line and are pushed down, but others should originate with employees themselves.

There are four kinds of objectives:

1 *Routine.* This is a continuation and extension of what people are already doing. "We sold 20,000 units last year. In order to preserve our share of the market and our profit margin, we need to sell 22,500 units this year." Everyone needs to work a bit more effectively, to improve over last year's output. There can be a challenge in that. But if every year you better the previous year, you come to expect it. Knowing that you can do it —in fact, that you have done it consistently—lowers the challenge. Too many routine goals cause the goal-setting process to lose its sparkle.

While it may be that employees have little to say about the quantity of work to be done, they may have much to say about how it is to be accomplished. "We have to produce 10 percent more this year with the same people and equipment. How do you think we can do it?" That kind of team effort can stimulate excitement.

2 *Problem solving.* "Our reject rate is 22 percent higher than it was during the same period last year. We have a problem. How can we solve it?" This is a necessity that is imposed from higher up, as management realizes how costly the increased reject rate is. Or, "Our audits show that errors in claims payments have jumped from 3 percent to 7 percent. How can we get this figure down?" You have a problem. It's time to consult the experts, the people who probably know more about the work than anyone else: the people who are doing it. From their counsel, you can help them to set goals involving solutions to the problem: "Okay, with the first steps you suggest, we can lower the rate to 5 percent in three months, then with the additional steps we can hit 3 percent in five months."

3 *Innovation.* Again, some of your subordinates are in a position to advise you on changes or projects that are new. They may be able to suggest them. But you probably can't initiate too many changes in a given time period. Excessive innovation would be a drain on your resources. If possible, each time period and each goal-setting session should see at least one innovation.

4 *Personal.* "What are you doing for you?" is a question that you as manager should be asking your subordinates. Or, even better, "What can we (the organization) be helping you to do for yourself?" Personal objectives should be part of the goal-setting process. They include training and education (seminars, courses, in-house), perhaps some job rotation and behavior—in short, improvements of technical skills and preparation for advancement.

Behavioral objectives can be set to increase the employee's effectiveness. For example, you might tell someone who must run meetings, "I think you would get a lot more out of the meetings you conduct if you could get more participation from your staff. Let's work on some techniques you might try to encourage people to open up more." Objectives that provide improvement of interpersonal skills are an essential part of the goal-setting process.

Setting the goals

Ideally, the process of setting goals should be a stimulating one for both manager and subordinate. Looking ahead and agreeing on what is important to be done should provide some excitement, especially if manager and subordinate are realistic, believe the objectives are relevant, and can find something in the objectives that relates personally.

If the objectives are realistic, they should then be nonthreatening. A goal-setting session ought to be an interesting and very natural occasion. In fact, people should look forward to it, if only because the process provides an opportunity to get together with the boss and talk about matters that are important to both of them. Of course, how openly they talk with the manager, how much information they volunteer, largely depends on the climate in the department. If they feel the atmosphere generally discourages being open and spontaneous, the manager can hardly expect a sudden change of behavior at goal-setting time.

To encourage subordinates to be relaxed, and to come to the session prepared to talk, you might consider these suggestions:

1 *Give advance notice.* People need time to think about what they regard as important. Unrealistic objectives often result when subordinates, without warning, have to come up with plans off the top of the head. Remind them that you want them to think about all four kinds of goals that I have just described.

2 *Provide essential information.* What changes are going to occur, or have occurred recently, that will change the nature and quantity of the objectives? What capital equipment will be added? Will a function be phased out or transferred to another department? What effects will a reorganization have on the amount and type of work? Are there personnel changes that will affect goals? What will be the impact of a new product that is to be introduced? What changes in the organizational structure or management or overall objectives should be considered in your departmental goal setting?

3 *Allow plenty of time for the meeting.* This is a prime time for both of you to learn what is on each other's mind. Also, the amount of time you set aside for the process is an indicator of how much importance you assign it. Managers who seem to begrudge the time, who rush through the process, broadcast that they don't grant much importance to setting goals. As I've already pointed out, the goal-setting interview gives you a chance to convey to employees what you expect of them. But it is equally valuable in letting you find out what objectives (and activities) are high on their lists. You may discover that the way they see their jobs is a far cry from the way you see them, and this is the time to cut down on that disparity.

Employees may bring problems to the meeting with you that you were only dimly aware of. They may suggest innovations that you hadn't thought of. And they may furnish you with some solid—and unexpected—clues as their personal career objectives, information that you can use in coaching at a later date. (See chapter 11.)

4 *State the goals.* Objectives should be stated clearly and concisely. For example, "Increase sales by 12 percent by December 31." "Have 50 percent of departmental personnel capable of using computer terminals by April 15." "Have round-the-clock telephone reporting system for claims by June 1." If there are very many, you may be well advised to assign priorities to them, unless, of course, employees are accustomed to a multitude of objectives and can be expected to give them all a fair shot.

How much time should you give to discussing the means by which the objectives are to be reached? Obviously, a discussion of means is important if the objectives are new, or at least are new to the employee. Some subordinates will value an extensive review of means with you more than others, while some will probably be more highly motivated if you leave a development of means to them.

In most cases, a brief action plan describing means is helpful. For example, if you have as an objective increasing the market share in a particular area, your action plan might go something like this: "We will supplement calls to dealers by a four-times-a-year mailing to large volume customers and prospects." Or if your goal is to reduce production costs: "Let's analyze overtime activities and costs, and schedule more work during regular hours."

5 *Get agreement on the goals.* Don't just assume

that employees accept and support your statement of goals—or priorities. Make sure, by asking them how they feel about each of the objectives. For your part, you can elaborate on how each of the goals relates to your own and the overall organizational goals. This may also be the time to show how each objective relates to the employee. What will the experience of achieving it mean to the subordinate? How will it contribute to his or her development, advancement, image, etc.? In short, do a bit of selling. Be prepared to show the benefits to the subordinate of a commitment to the goals. You may want to consult chapter 7 on ways to make the work more valuable.

6 *Make sure the employee understands how the achievement will be measured.* Set up the subgoals and the time period. Remember that it is helpful for the employee to see progress. Too long a period between setting the goal and measuring progress toward it can rob the goal of its importance and the employee of enthusiasm for achieving it. "We should have achieved one-fourth of the objective by March 1. We'll talk then, see how we're doing, and adjust if necessary. We may find that the final goal should be higher, or lower, although I hope not."

I firmly believe that discussions of progress, especially the final one, should be tied in with appraisal of performance. And that relationship is dealt with in greater depth in chapter 10.

7 *Follow-up in writing.* First of all, it serves as a reminder. But just as important, your written follow-up ensures that you and the subordinate have agreed on the same things. The employee should understand that if there is a disparity, you want to hear about it immediately.

Incidentally, all of these procedures can be followed when groups, as well as individuals, set goals, which many management experts feel should be done as often as possible. Group goal setting can take the place of much of the individual goal setting, or can supplement it. Naturally, personal objectives should be discussed individually.

Each goal-setting session, then, should cover all four areas. Each session should include objectives that come down from above and those that originate in the department and with individual employees. The follow-through has to be conscientious, even scrupulous. And when the goal is reached, the accomplishment has to be recognized. Year in, year out. It never ceases. That's the only way a manager can clearly deliver the message, "These goals are important—to me, to you."

6: Matching personal goals with the work

There is no way that you can hope to set goals or assign tasks effectively without having a sense of subordinates' *personal* goals. Indeed, a sense may be all you have. People are not always eager to reveal to others, especially to you the boss, what makes them go. (That's certainly true if what makes them go is that they would like to replace you.) And many people are not always aware of the motivating forces in them and the direction in which they are moving.

But, as I've pointed out, you can be sure that people do what they do for specific reasons, even if they keep them to themselves. If those reasons or goals can be satisfied through accomplishment of both the organization's and your own objectives, then you'll have a committed employee (though not always an effective one, since the ability to perform is as important as the will).

There are employees who are working to be able to afford material goods or a certain lifestyle. The work itself may always be of secondary interest, but that does not necessarily mean that they don't do it well. Quite the contrary. This person is interested in doing well enough to earn raises and to achieve job security. However, since this employee looks for challenge and fulfillment away from the job, he or she is usually reluctant to take on complicated new responsibilities or substantial risks that may threaten the situation as it is now. You would be ill-advised to push such a person in a new direction without minimizing the consequences of failure.

Some people look to work to help satisfy their need to belong—what psychologists call social or affiliation needs. They work well and conscientiously in groups, less efficiently in tasks that require them to be apart from others. (For example, people with strong social needs often make poor outside salespeople.) It's difficult to make airtight generalizations, but it is frequently true that strong joiners accept the values of the work group of which they are members. Thus, they will become involved with the boss's objectives if that's where the energies of the group are directed. Unfortunately, it works the other way, too. You may find, therefore, that this person must be approached through the work group, not directly. That is, you think of the kind of work or task to which the entire group would respond.

Other personal goals

Esteem—their own and others'—is something many people work to achieve. Your esteem might be valuable to subordinates, and for a time at least, or on certain tasks, they will invest themselves to earn it. The chief point to remember is that people who work for esteem usually accept challenge and risk that are moderate. They need achievement in order to earn that esteem. If the risk is too low, they'll discount it or pass it up. But they aren't necessarily gamblers, willing to take the plunge for a big payoff when the odds are against them.

Esteem-seekers often are competitive—moderately so. They want more than to be accepted by others; they want respect, and that often can be gained by winning over others. Therefore, this person will usually seek achievement and responsibility. But he or she is not a jungle fighter, not so competitive that in beating out others, the employee alienates them. On the other hand, the person who is strongly motivated by self-esteem needs may be willing to succeed even though the price is offending others.

There are people who move toward power. They tend to be political and to take risks where they believe there is a reasonable chance for payoff. These people may commit themselves to do whatever they see as required to gain responsibility and influence over others. So long as they work for you, they will probably be among your best subordinates. But bear in mind that they will probably not long be content to work for you. Moreover, not all power-seekers are high performers. Some are empire-builders, which takes a lot of energy. They work to acquire people, equipment, space, and prestige, and what it takes to do all of that may detract from their effectiveness in seeking your objectives.

There is a power-seeker of a different kind who may prove to be a continuing asset to you: the employee who is seeking personal power or freedom. I equate the two because they have much in common. Having power means having options, choices. Having freedom means much the same thing. This kind of employee wants freedom over work, the opportunity to choose the kind of work done and the means to do it. A strict bureaucratic boss may have problems with the personal power-seeker, but most managers who can delegate and let employees off the leash will find this person to be a joy.

Mixed in with all of these other motivations is the need to achieve. It is strong in many people. It leads to self-esteem, the respect of others, promotion, power, money, and, not the least, satisfaction with oneself. The true achiever needs change, challenge, and moderate risk. (The person who seeks exceptional risk is usually the entrepreneur, and as such, may not be a good subordinate for you.) One sure way to de-motivate a high achiever is to keep that person in the same job for years.

Unfortunately many high achievers do get stuck. Some managers do not seem to realize that approximately all 80 percent of jobs can be learned within two to three years. After that, the employee is overlearning, expending a great deal of energy for relatively little return. Successful salespeople are the most frequent victims of overlearning. They become burned out, to the astonishment of their managers. Once at a talk I delivered to sales managers, I was asked, "How do you motivate a salesman who was a big producer for several years but now is on a plateau? He turns in just enough business to stay on the job." I asked the manager how long the salesman had been doing essentially the same thing. The answer was ten years. My response was a question: "How much enthusiasm would *you* have for doing the same thing for ten years?" Few people would continue to be high producers under such conditions.

Many of us are self-actualizers, to borrow from Maslow. Probably most of us are to some extent. We are impelled to become increasingly what we are capable of being. Sometimes we may not be clear as to what this is. Or we may be reluctant to be open with others about our life's dreams and goals. But the drives are there, and we look for goals that will help us satisfy these needs.

Discovering others' goals

Discovering others' goals often isn't easy; what complicates the issue is that there are about as many kinds of goals as there are people to set them. Still, the manager who recognizes that people have needs that they try to satisfy on the job, even if not always aware of the precise nature of those needs, is usually far ahead of the manager who fails to take employees' needs into account when assigning work, providing training, and rewarding accomplishment.

What about the manager who really doesn't want to know employees' specific goals? Some managers believe that it's an invasion of privacy to try to get that kind of information out of their employees. But you don't have to delve that deeply. You don't have to pry. Just don't ignore the motivations that are rooted in personal needs.

One manager I know resolves the privacy issue by periodically giving employees a piece of paper divided into two sections. The top half is for the employee to spell out, in private, those things that the employee wants to achieve through the work. For example, "I want to make a lot of money"; or, "I want to be manager of the engineering department"; or, "I'd like to complete my education in chemistry and transfer to R&D." There may be any number of personal objectives that the employee can define.

The bottom half is for the employee to list the kinds of work, tasks, activities that would contribute to the satisfaction of the needs, the achievement of the goals in the top half of the form. The manager instructs the employee to tear off the goals section and keep it. The bottom half is to be discussed with the manager, if the employee is willing to share. The manager then takes the information into account when planning work, training, etc.

This can be an effective approach for the manager who is reluctant to get involved in discussions of those needs and goals that the employee may be more comfortable keeping to himself or herself. For the manager who does want to encourage employees to open up, the key word is *trust*. If you want the employee to be genuine about personal objectives, you have to be extremely careful never to appear to use the information in any way but respectfully. One manager told me of the time he met with an older boss some years back. The senior manager wanted to know in what direction the young man was moving. So the young man opened up, only to have the manager snort and say, "Now that's foolish. What you really should be thinking more about is . . ." And then the manager talked for several minutes about what he thought the younger man's objectives should be.

Accept what you hear, even if you don't agree with it. The important thing is that the other person believes it, takes it seriously. You can take it seriously as well, even if you don't think it is realistic. Here's a technique for responding with an evaluation of goals that is quite different from the one the employee has offered: "It's interesting that you say this. I would have thought, from observing and working with you, that you might have felt differently." Then offer your opinions.

Obviously, don't even appear to take what you hear lightly, even if you do find the employee's revelations about self quite at odds with your evaluation. And make every effort to keep the information to yourself, or if it must be shared, be as discreet as possible. For the employee to hear something from a third party or through the grapevine that he or she thought was to be treated confidentially is to invite a personal vote of no-confidence.

There are a number of questions that the manager can ask to elicit information that will help in matching personal and organizational objectives. For example:

What aspects of the job do you like most? Least?

What functions would you like to spend more time doing, if you could? Less time doing?

What kinds of tasks are you not doing now that you would like to do, if you had the opportunity?

What kinds of work and responsibilities do you see yourself performing or having in three to five years?

All of the above questions can be useful in encouraging a person to think specifically about how the job can offer opportunities to satisfy personal needs and goals. In rare cases, they may also uncover a frustration deriving from the knowledge that the job really can't offer satisfaction. If you have an employee who seems to have the ability but just isn't performing according to your standards, this revelation may prompt you to suggest that the person go elsewhere as he or she is not likely to find satisfaction in this job situation.

More frequently, the manager can alter duties and

responsibilities to bring the job more closely to what the employee needs and wants. Perhaps some of the job can be transferred to a co-worker who would value it more, or some duties might be exchanged. It is seldom that nothing can be done to enhance the person's belief that many of his or her personal needs can be met through the job.

One additional exercise that takes time but produces valuable data is this: "Describe in detail what your work would be like, would consist of, if you had the job you consider ideal? How would you spend your time?" Not only does the exercise open a window for the manager, it sometimes helps employees to realize that present conditions are much closer to the ideal than they thought.

Your own observations will supplement the information that the employee offers. Your records should show areas of achievement and patterns of successful behavior, should point to strengths and weaknesses. Your knowledge of your employees should suggest to you which people show enthusiasm for what kinds of work. I maintain that there is usually a strong correlation between what people do well over time and what they prefer to do.

Your knowledge of people's preferences, needs, and goals can help you in assigning them to tasks and jobs in which they will feel more satisfied and will probably perform more effectively. You want them to value what they are doing so that they will see advantages to them in doing the work well. The information you receive from them and derive from observation can help you to anticipate how they see the chance of being successful in certain kinds of work. You will have important clues to what kinds of situations the employee performs better in.

In short, your management efforts will go with the grain.

Douglas McGregor, you'll recall, wrote in his Theory

Y: "Man will exercise self-direction and self-control in the service of objectives to which he is committed." And he also wrote, "Commitment to objectives is a function of the rewards associated with achievement of those objectives."

7: Making the job more valuable

You can increase the value of a job or assignment to an employee by offering rewards for doing it—and for doing it well. Unfortunately, when it comes to rewards for good performance, managers spend far too much time thinking about money. Or the lack of it. True, money can be an effective motivator; it can add much value to a task. Almost everyone appreciates a monetary reinforcer. Recently I was talking with a television personality about a series of programs he had done. He winced and said, "I don't know why I did those shows." Then he laughed, "Oh yes, I do. It was the money."

Managers frequently ask me whether I believe the surveys that purport to show that, when people are asked to rank those factors that motivate them, they almost invariably put money after several other motivators. (Interestingly, when managers are asked to rank what they believe motivates subordinates, the resulting lists usually place money at or near the top.) Yes, I believe them. People are too complicated and individual for all of them to be motivated so strongly by the same material thing. Furthermore, if such surveys do nothing else, they show that subordinates accept reality more readily than their bosses: Few people in organizations will ever make sufficient money so that it becomes a powerful motivator.

Money, especially a great deal of it, can make a job more pleasant or meaningful. And money is an indicator of one's worth to the organization. It confers status. A high income helps a person do and buy things that may help that person tolerate a less-than-ideal job. Money may also reinforce the competitiveness that seems to drive so many people. It is recognition; it confirms one's sense of achievement.

But most managers don't have a lot of money at their disposal. Organizational wage-and-salary policies limit the amount they can give employees. And the way most employers give money as a reward erodes its effectiveness: once a year and long after the fact. Promotions fall in the same category as money—powerful motivators but not always available. Too, unlike money, not everyone responds to the prospect of being promoted.

While money and promotions are the most obvious rewards, you may be surprised at the variety of other reinforcers you have available. Most managers are quite surprised, when they start thinking about it, to find out just how many rewards they actually have available to make work more valuable to subordinates. As you read, you may want to develop your own list for future use.

While there are many reinforcers, there are two basic types: internal and external. You can enhance the former and grant the latter.

Internal rewards

Internal reinforcers are generated within the person. Employees give themselves their own rewards. For example, Herzberg talks about achievement and progress, reinforcers that occur when the person has reached a goal, whether it is set by the person or by the organization. Because the reinforcement comes from within the person, a manager may think, "Well, there's not much I can do about it." That's one mistake. Another error a manager may fall into is not believing that employees must have their sense of achievements reinforced. You might overhear one such manager saying, "She's a pro.

She knows better than anyone else when she does a good job." Believing this, the manager loses a valuable opportunity to enhance the good feelings that the achiever has.

There are at least two steps a manager can take to increase the value of internally generated rewards. The first is one that I discussed in a previous chapter: helping to establish attainable goals and measurements so that achievement is evident. The manager takes the second step by helping the employee to recognize that there are internal rewards for accomplishment. He or she gives the employee something to look forward to. For example, a subordinate is going through an extensive and difficult breaking-in period. The manager might say something such as, "I know it's tough going now, but once you've gotten through it, you'll find that you'll have a different feeling about the job. You'll be more relaxed, much more confident about your ability to take on almost any situation."

The manager might also add the likelihood that the employee will take a great deal of pleasure in being able to perform confidently. The subordinate just might *like* the job more—and that's no insignificant reinforcer.

The following are examples of how a manager can anticipate and highlight those internal rewards that an achieving or well-performing subordinate deserves:

A sense of growth. "I'm sure this experience that you're accumulating will give you a sense of the progress you're making."

Status. "The way you're expanding your know-how, you'll probably be the most versatile person in this department."

Achievement. "If you keep this pace up, you will be the first person in this region ever to fill the annual quota by May."

Self-esteem. When you know how important it is to an employee to feel skilled or professional, you can point out how certain kinds of tasks, training, and experiences can lead to this heightened sense of worth. "You're going to feel increasingly valuable to this department."

Social needs. It is important for most people to be accepted as members of the group. A manager can subtly reinforce these desires by suggesting ways in which an employee, through achievement, acquisition of skills, changes of behavior, can increase that acceptance by others. Peer approval and acceptance of others on the work scene can meet many of a person's social needs. "I've been hearing from some of your co-workers some good words about how skilled you are getting to be in running the scheduling sessions."

As manager, you must not assume that employees automatically reinforce themselves when they do well. Ironically, they may not have the sense of achievement that you think they have when they have reached an objective. You are in a position to help them to define what has to be done and to recognize when they have, in fact, done it.

External rewards

When you call attention to a job well done, you can not only enhance the person's feeling of achievement and satisfaction but also provide reinforcement of your own. Your reinforcement is, of course, external.

Usually the most desirable and potent reward is an internal reinforcer backed up by one that is external. As I've suggested, there are many kinds of external rewards. Three that are usually readily available to you are: 1. More work; 2. Training; and 3. More of you.

Most managers I talk with find the list amusing— initially. Although we are not accustomed to thinking of any of the three as rewards for good performance, when explained, they all make very good sense.

More work doesn't mean piling on more duties. It does

mean more challenging work, more responsibility, more of what the employee would like to do.

Training usually carries a negative connotation. If I say that I think you need more training, you may hear me suggesting that you have a deficiency that training will make up. To think of training as a reward is new to many.

More of you seems to represent a contradiction. Good performers usually need less supervision, not more. But you as a manager certainly have more to offer than your supervisory function.

Each of these three deserves a closer look.

MORE WORK

Herzberg regards the work itself as a motivator. If it is, and if it is successfully done, then more work might be a reinforcer. Of course, the message shouldn't be, "Around here, if you do a good job, they pile on more work." The work should be interesting and challenging, something that an employee prizes. The assignment should be accompanied by the message, "Because you handled Task A so well, I want to expand your experience and responsibility by letting you have a crack at Task B." If you pull down Task B from a higher level of authority and responsibility than the subordinate is normally entitled to, you are, in Herzberg's terms, enriching his or her job. It's called *vertical loading.* You are loading the subordinate's job with responsibilities from the next one or two levels above.

For example, start with yourself. What are some of the functions you perform that you prize, that you enjoy doing? Would some of them be appropriate to delegate? For example, you do the assignments for the department. You like the job. You pride yourself on your skillful matching of ability and needs. This job is one you might consider training an outstanding performer to do. Or, you do spot checking of the output. Choose a good worker to do your checking for you.

A committee or task force is an enriching tool that too few managers consider. One manager did—and quite successfully. Realizing that too little planning went on in her operation, she set up a task force of her superior performers to develop a list of possible future projects. They were to estimate the feasibility of each, then develop priorities. Over time the task force worked up action plans for the higher priority projects. Eventually, some of these were implemented, headed up in many cases by the members of the task force that had conceived them.

A task force can provide a stretching experience for your good performers. At the very least, it is a change of pace from the daily routine. At the most, it is highly stimulating to sit together with other people who are superior performers to solve a significant problem or to launch a project. Being appointed to such a group broadcasts to everyone that the employee is well regarded by management. What comes out of the project—a new program or even a product—can continue the reinforcement for years, if it endures and is successful. (See chapter 17 for a more complete description of this underutilized job-enrichment and training tool.)

Not everyone will be motivated to undertake more responsibility. But chances are there are people who report to you who are not getting what they can and want to handle.

You can do much to provide more satisfying work for your superior subordinates by finding out what they like to do best and providing more opportunities for them to do it. For instance, the last time you hired a new administrative assistant, you asked Margaret to take responsibility for integrating her into the department and speeding up the time when she would be effective. Margaret did the job well. In recognition, you might ask her to recommend other areas and people for training.

TRAINING

Surprisingly little recognition is given to the fact that people want to grow. Training and education can help people to develop their potential. Unfortunately, as I pointed out, training often carries with it a slight suggestion of inadequacy. One reason for this is the practice in many organizations of diagnosing needs and then prescribing training to meet them. That's a valid approach; but if it is the only approach, training is unlikely to be seen as a reinforcer. For example, at a recent Assertiveness Training for Managers workshop, many attendees candidly reported that they were there because their bosses perceived them as either abrasive or nonassertive. They had come to be corrected, to move closer to what their bosses thought they ought to be.

In contrast, a short time later I sat in on another three-day workshop on communicating skills—both business writing and speaking in public. Many employees would not find this training essential to the performance of their responsibilities. But since almost everyone values these skills, imagine how a valued employee might feel if the boss said, "I know of a good workshop on speaking skills. Someday being able to get up before a group and speak well on your feet might be useful. If you'd like to go, I'll foot the bill."

Most training and education is seen as work-related. That's understandable. But don't rule out courses, seminars, workshops, and lectures that broaden the perspective and deepen the thinking of the participants, even if they don't contribute to everyday effectiveness on the job. And the more personal the benefit, the greater the probability that the experience will be seen as a reward and will reinforce. Moreover, if there is a sequence to the training, that would indicate progress and more responsibility. That is, each training segment would lead to more responsibility, and good performance in that responsibility would in turn result in more training. For example, a manager on a marketing track who had gone from field management of salespeople to forecasting and EDP would certainly perceive a direction and advancement in the data-processing and quantitative decision-making courses.

How employees see training and educational opportunities depends in large part on how the manager presents them. If they are provided out of a need, let the need be that of the department. For the valued employee whose performance the manager wishes to reward, the opportunity should clearly benefit the person.

MORE OF YOU

Yes, you can be a reward. For example, your esteem could be very important to a subordinate. If you assign a job that you regard as special, don't miss the opportunity to let your subordinate know that your esteem of his or her ability is what led you to make the assignment.

You might also consider that an employee will view freer access to you as a recognition of that person's value to you. Managers have ways of letting it be known that, even though their schedules are crowded, they can usually find time for certain people. That access, incidentally, doesn't have to be strictly formal or one-way. Some managers make it a practice to drop by subordinates' offices, desks, or work stations for a short chat when neither is under pressure. Those informal occasions with better-performing employees constitute a clear message to them and to others.

One way to increase access and express esteem is by consulting with key people. The manager periodically says to a valued subordinate, "I wanted to get your opinion on something." It may be an incipient project, a potential new employee, a restructuring of the department, or some aspect of office decoration. The opinions don't all have to be adopted, but they must be sincerely sought.

Do you occasionally sit down with a subordinate you

regard highly and offer career counseling? If you do, then you're not surprised that employees value your interest and advice. Most of us in organizations don't get as much help in planning our careers as we need. You occupy a vantage point. You know more than your subordinates about what is happening or about to happen in the organization, the opportunities that are opening up, prerequisites for promotion and certain kinds of jobs, and the career paths that have proved to be most promising.

Finally, there is your concern. You can express it on a professional level by giving career advice, telling the employee, "Your work is of such quality that I regard you as an asset to this organization. I would like to suggest ways in which you can become more valuable to you and to us."

Your concern can also be expressed on the personal level. "Look, you've been working awfully hard lately. Why don't you knock off early on Friday and enjoy a long weekend."

A SAMPLING OF REWARDS

Most managers, when they think about it, are astonished at the number of rewards that are available to them. Some representative reinforcers:

1 *More desirable workplace.* Yes, of course, the corner office. But it can be less elaborate—a new desk or chair, a rug, or a different location. First choice goes to the better performers.

2 *Recognition.* People who accomplish in a superior manner usually like the fact to be known—by memo, a notice on the bulletin board, a letter to your manager, or even higher up. Perhaps an article in the organization publication.

Keep in mind that praise is a powerful form of recognition. It doesn't have to cost anything. It doesn't always have to be public. You can bestow it privately.

Praise has to be given carefully if it is to produce the desired consequences. Because praise is a potent and yet complicated reinforcer, it is dealt with more extensively later in the book.

3 *More freedom.* One subordinate is given the chance to set his own hours or work schedule. Another, a valued supervisor, told me that her boss doesn't maintain a strict vacation record on her. She is trusted not to abuse the privilege. The chance to do office work at home now and then is prized by many. One specialist who formerly had her work reviewed by her boss now has it checked by another on her level. The results are approximately the same, but the message of trust—in both—is a clear reinforcer.

Providing more freedom for an employee is a reinforcer too little utilized by managers. That is surprising, especially in view of the fact that many good performers have demonstrated their ability to work without close supervision. Making it official is a message that will be understood and appreciated. The privileges don't have to be extensive; they do, however, have to be seen, not as lax management or indifference, but as a reward for service.

4 *Equipment.* A more elaborate calculator, a more expensive typewriter, a two-line phone, a nightline for use after the switchboard has closed down. Ask yourself, "What kind of equipment will make this person's job easier?"

5 *Opportunity to represent you.* Give a valuable employee a chance to chair a meeting for you—or to represent you at a meeting you can't attend. Offer the subordinate that trip to San Francisco or New York that you would usually take.

Some managers seem to have what I consider to be an inordinate fear of favoritism. But I am convinced that a manager should accord special treatment to those employees who perform well and willingly to achieve organizational objectives. What people have done and are doing count. That certain employees may be likable or relate well to the manager or have attractive personalities or be popular with other employees does not count when it comes to favorable treatment. If the manager is careful to extend special consideration to those employees who do a good job, and to limit such consideration to that group, then he or she will clearly convey the message, "This is what I do for people who perform well. Do a good job, and you will enjoy the same benefits." That kind of favoritism clearly works in the manager's favor.

Being specific

What I have been discussing are ways a manager can increase the value of work for subordinates through both internal and external rewards. It is not always necessary—and not always desirable—to promise these reinforcers in advance, or to be specific about what kind of reward may follow specific performance. What is essential is that subordinates see the reinforcements as a consequence of their own good performance or others'. They need to be able to say to themselves, "If I do well, the boss will recognize it." Gradually people learn that commitment to and achievement of your objectives will be rewarded.

But when should you be clear about the reward you intend to grant following a certain performance? One recommended occasion is the assignment of an especially difficult or unpopular task, something that you know the employee will do but not with great willingness. "Look, I know that you're not terribly enthusiastic about doing this, but I'd like you to do it. I'll make a point of pushing for a special raise for you." Or, "I know how much you want to go to that meeting in San Francisco. You have my support." Or, you may wish to combine an undesired task with one that is highly desirable.

"You've been wanting to do that study of our sales compensation system. Take on this job, and I'll get you approval for your study."

Another time you may want to be specific about the reward is when you know the kind of reinforcement the person seeks. One brilliant young mathematician who wanted a division managership was persuaded to stay in the home office for another year doing complex decision models for the computer with the prospect of getting not only the division he sought, but the title of vice-president.

A third opportunity for specificity is when you know that a particular kind of performance will qualify the subordinate for the reward. "This will add to your qualifications for membership in the association, and, of course, we'll pick up your membership fee."

Being specific can help you to get special effort from people. What is essential is that you be sure that the reward that you specify will, in fact, follow the performance, and that both you and the subordinate are very clear about the level of performance that you require.

In short, when you promise or even suggest a specific reward, you must know the person and what he or she regards as a reward, and you must be reasonably sure that you can deliver.

8: Helping them believe they can

No matter how attractive a goal is, no matter how desirable a reward is, most people are not likely to try for it unless they see a reasonable chance that they will reach it. Their perceptions, their expectations of success are what matter. As a manager, you may feel that at times you have to be almost psychic to judge how employees feel about their ability to do a job or assignment. You hope that they'll tell you how they perceive their chances of success. Sometimes they don't.

An experienced writer and editor joined the periodicals division in a publishing company. Because of his experience, and because the division was understaffed, he was quickly appointed managing editor of an important monthly trade publication. He seemed to relish the new opportunity and showed pride in winning the responsibility so soon after joining the staff. After a time, contributors to the publication that he managed began to complain about the fact that some of their work never appeared in print. The managing editor seemed reluctant to give them a status report on their articles. The publisher became unhappy with the layout. Pages were made up awkwardly, often cluttered.

The managing editor became defensive about the criticism, once showed up at a staff meeting with a long, self-conscious justification of the way he ran the publication. Eventually he began to call in sick. He was prone to accidents. Something always seemed to interfere with his ability to do a good job. Management became deeply concerned and faced the possibility that the managing editor would have to be fired. Finally, one executive said, "Perhaps he is in over his head and is afraid to admit it." Acting on the suggestion, the publisher of the trade publication announced that he was assuming a new role, that of executive editor. The managing editor would continue to run the publication, but final editorial approval would come from the executive editor/publisher.

Not only did the managing editor not resent the new reporting relationship, he seemed to thrive on it. Ultimate responsibility was lifted from his shoulders. He appeared to welcome having someone check his work and provide a backstop. The publication showed marked improvement. The managing editor became more confident, less defensive.

The diagnosis had been correct. The managing editor had sought the responsibility, yet early on had begun to doubt that he could handle it. Performance and quality dropped.

Avoiding assumptions

Too often, managers remain unaware of subordinates' opinions that a particular job or function presents difficulties. In making assignments, or at the first sign of performance problems in a job, managers should be careful not to assume that employees will volunteer that they are worried about their ability to do the job.

Sitting back, assuming that employees will sound an alarm, is only one mistake a manager can make. There are other assumptions that can get managers into trouble. For example, there's little to be gained by a manager thinking, "Sam has always done well at this, so there's no reason why he won't now"; or, "Sheila ought to be able to tackle this with the training we've provided"; or, "If I were in Fred's shoes, I could do it with one arm tied behind my back." The question isn't whether the manager feels the employee can do well—

or ought to. There may be good reasons for the manager to believe that employees are capable of doing a good job. The only thing that matters is whether *they*, the employees, believe that the job or task is doable. Subordinates might see a number of variables or obstacles that the manager hasn't considered.

The best time to deal with an employee's low probability of success is before the work is undertaken. If you suspect that an employee is floundering in a job, or less than enthusiastic about finishing—or even taking on— an assignment, consider asking questions that will uncover an employee's hesitancy or concern. For example: Do you foresee—or are you running into—any problems doing this work? What, in your opinion, is the best way to go about this task? Is there anything I, or anyone else, can do to help you to do a more successful job? Do you feel that there are obstacles to your doing a better job that we might be able to get rid of?

For more serious cases, you might wish to refer to the counseling or coaching techniques described in later chapters.

There are steps you should almost always take in assigning a task or job that will help increase the employee's expectation of achieving success:

1 *Define the task* as precisely as necessary. While there may be nothing extraordinary in this counsel, there's really nothing ordinary in it either. It just isn't done as often as it should be. One of the most common managerial failings is taking for granted that the other person knows what the manager wants. And one of the most common reasons that people see difficulties in performing is that they're not sure what is to be done.

If you're not clear about what you hope to wind up with, be prepared for almost anything.

Think in terms of goals—as specifically as possible. Goals are output. It isn't enough to say, "We're launching a new print advertising campaign and we want you to be responsible for handling the inquiries as they come in."

What does "handle" mean? To this manager, it means that the subordinate is supposed to organize and train a group of people to acknowledge by mail the nearly ten thousand prospect inquiry cards that are expected, and to organize those cards by sales districts so that they can be sent to field reps who will then call on the prospects personally.

To talk in terms of responsibility for something usually means the input required, not the output or the results.

It's strange how many people are infected with input-itis. Anyone who reads resumes of job applicants knows that they often tell you, somewhat vaguely, that they were responsible in a previous job for implementing something or another, but they don't tell you what happened as a result of it. If an applicant says that she was responsible for designing orientation and training programs for all secretaries hired by the corporation, she hasn't told much of anything. What she should describe is how extensive the programs were, how many people were put through them, what they were able to do at the conclusion of the orientation and training that they probably weren't able to do before, and so on. Then she is more likely to impress.

Managers suffer from input-itis as well. Remember that, in assigning tasks or jobs, you should talk as specifically as possible about what you expect to be done. It will give you a better chance of clearing up any anxieties or doubts in employees' minds about their abilities to do what you want. At the least, it will encourage employees to talk about specific aspects of the goal that may trouble them. For example, "Well, I can see acknowledging the inquiries, but I'm not sure how we can district the cards for salespeople. Where can we get the geographical breakdown?"

When you have a long-range goal, especially one

that is complex, break it down into subgoals. "I want us to put out 5,000 units this year. I realize that we have to gear up, train people, get the bugs out. So our subgoal is 800 in the first quarter, 2,000 in the second, etc." Breaking the task down into smaller units lessens the enormity or complexity in the doer's mind.

2 *Set standards.* Tell *how* the job is to be done. I hear managers report how they hand job descriptions to employees, insisting that is all that is necessary. But job descriptions don't usually convey standards.

One unfortunate middle-aged manager took over a department from another manager who had been promoted. He knew the work, had done it before. He was also acquainted with the position description. Yet, after about one year, he was called into the office of his immediate superior and told that his work was unacceptable. He was mystified. He thought he had been doing a good job. No one had told him differently. Now he found himself in danger of being fired.

If you assign that job of "handling" the reader inquiries, tell the subordinate how well you would like it done. For example, "I'd like to see all inquiries acknowledged by return mail—or at least within twenty-four hours. I would hope that the districting of inquiries could be completed within forty-eight hours. We're alerting the reps that they can expect a new batch of leads every three or four days, certainly once a week."

That spells out how you expect the job to be done. You've also stated what you consider to be minimally acceptable standards: ". . . at least within twenty-four hours," and the reps should receive leads no less than once each week.

Standards include a time frame—so much activity within a certain period of time. The manager doesn't usually forget to specify the time frame on short-term or repetitive functions: ten units in eight hours. But on tasks that will take longer, it's a good idea to spell out how long you think it should take. You may think in terms of six months, while the subordinate worries that you may want it in six weeks. Furthermore, indicate how rigid or flexible the time period is. Knowing that the schedule can be extended, if necessary, may be sufficient to ease any problems an employee foresees in doing the work.

3 *Describe the resources available.* Telling subordinates about what help there is available to them can go far to allay doubt or fears that they can't succeed in doing the kind of job they and you want. For example:

> *Authority.* If you're going to define responsibility, it's only fair to tell the subordinate how much authority he or she will have in order to do the job. How many people will be reporting to the subordinate? For how long? Will the reporting be full—or part time? What decisions can be made by the subordinate? Does the subordinate have the power to hire, fire, transfer, or discipline?
>
> *People.* Where are the people to come from? For example, you might say to your supervisor of inquiry responses, "Talk to Ed Peabody in personnel and discuss what you need with him," or, "Call the Temporary Help service. We'll use temps for this job." If the subordinate will be sharing employees with another manager—as in the case of a task force or other part-time assignment—you may have to lend a hand in the negotiation process with the other manager.
>
> *Equipment.* What office or production equipment will be needed? How should the employee go about getting it? Will access to a computer be useful? Perhaps you can't make a complete inventory in advance, but your assurances that reasonable equipment needs will be met can contribute much to an employee's confidence in a successful performance.
>
> *Facilities.* Where can the work be done? Will the conference room be available for meetings? Should the

office layout be rearranged to provide groupings of employees? A manager might say, "There's a spare area on the second floor where your team can put together a prototype. It's well lighted and secure."

Experts. You may wish to refer subordinates to advisors or consultants in personnel, training, marketing, research, both from inside and outside the organization. The subordinate and/or you will probably be billed for services, so explain any limitations and procedures in advance. There may be other employees or managers who are experienced in the kind of work you want done, and you can steer your subordinates to them for consultation and guidance. Or you may be that expert resource.

Precedents and guidelines. "Two years ago we did a similar readers' inquiry program. I think you'll find a file drawer with some samples of the acknowledgment we used, memos on how we got organized. It also seems to me that, after the whole thing, we put down on paper some suggestions for avoiding the mistakes we made." Experience of others in similar jobs or tasks can be an encouraging launching pad. Your own experience can help you develop guidelines and suggestions. Naturally you don't want to spell everything out so completely that there's no challenge, there's no room for the subordinate to bring his or her special talents to bear on the job. But you do want to make sure that the subordinate knows all of the resources, including and especially you, that are available.

Special efforts to increase probability

When you detect a reservation in an employee about the chances of successfully performing an assignment, or when you see signs of de-motivation because of fear of failure, you may want to take one or more of the following steps to bolster self-confidence:

1 *Relief from other duties.* Sometimes the em-

ployee doesn't consider the individual assignment too difficult, but the total workload does look formidable. State your priorities. "If you have too much on your plate, I'll understand. I'll lighten it. But the things that really count right now are . . ."

2 *Offer to collaborate.* You upgrade yourself from a resource to an active partner. There may be times when your experience, skills, and knowledge are needed, or would really push the project along. The problem is that it is hard for an employee to see you as an equal partner. Furthermore, you would be seen as getting the most glory, simply because you are more visible. At the same time, your presence on the task gives it more importance and prestige. A possible middle course for you is to say, "You and I will work together until you have things under control. Then you're on your own." Or, "Thereafter I'll come in only when you want." The implication is that you'll let the subordinate have the greater sense of achievement and most of the glory.

3 *Provide protection.* You take care of any interference from others that might hamper your subordinate. For example, in one department the supervisors freely called upon one another to help when the workload of one became excessive. It was a workable way of keeping the load fairly distributed. One supervisor received a special assignment from her boss, and at the same time was approached by another supervisor for help. In this case the boss took over the supervisor's obligation to provide help.

There are other more complex situations in which you might be called upon to protect your subordinate from outside interference—a higher manager who tends to bypass you to deal directly with your subordinates, a manager from another department who revives an off-and-on conflict with your subordinate. You may have to publicize the special authority you have given the subordinate, as in the case of a task force assignment in which the subordinate is negotiating with other managers for the time of certain of their employees.

Protection of employees from distracting events and outside people is one of the most important functions of a manager—all of the time. It is especially vital in the case of a special assignment that takes the employee somewhat out of the usual, predictable duties.

4 *Remove organizational barriers.* In most organizations what is called horizontal communication is weak. Employees often find communicating and cooperating across functional lines of authority difficult, primarily because the authority is different. It seems so easy to pick up the phone to say to a colleague in a different department reporting to a different boss, "Hey, Mike, we've had a rush request. How about shortcutting the paperwork on it and I'll get the papers to you day after tomorrow." Mike says he'll do it if the boss approves. So, you have to get an okay from Mike's supervisor.

If there is going to be a chain of requests such as this, you may be able to set up some special arrangements with the other department head so that your subordinate doesn't have to call for approval each time. You may have to be explicit about how far the arrangements go: "If you see a time problem developing, then you should call Mike, explain it, and . . . But only on this particular assignment."

5 *Provide training.* This, of course, is the most obvious step to take when an employee seems hesitant of his or her ability to do the job according to standards or expectations. That's the problem: It is obvious. Training is so easy to obtain. Training is often recommended when training isn't indicated. One sales manager I know frequently resorted to refresher training for his field force. He knew he had problems—poor compensation formulas, high turnover among field managers resulting in poor supervision, inadequate service and backup by the home office—but he seemed not to want to face them. In order to boost sagging morale among salespeople, he called them in for training. Eventually the point-lessness of the training became clear to everyone, except the sales manager who continued to plan more of it. Much managerial philosophy is based on this statement: When you don't know what else to do, train.

But there are times when specific skills need sharpening, knowledge and experience need deepening. Often the subordinate will indicate areas of deficiency: "Here's a three-day workshop on Management By Objectives. Do we have money in the budget to cover it?" Incidentally, it doesn't hurt to encourage the employee to tell you why he or she believes this training will be effective. For example, you might say, "Well, I agree that this looks interesting. What are some of the things about this workshop that you think might be of benefit to you?"

Training doesn't have to be formal and off-premises. You might be able to arrange for some coaching sessions with another manager. Sitting with a more experienced person can be useful. In fact, one of the most effective training programs I ever observed was little more than rotation of trainees throughout a division. The trainees themselves determined when they were ready for training in a particular function, then negotiated with the appropriate department head for the training time. During that time the trainee would work beside the manager or with section heads.

6 *Coach.* Some timely coaching may be called for, especially when a subordinate becomes almost overwhelmed by a feeling of inadequacy or incompetence. Many people have these feelings when they confront a task that is different from what they've been accustomed to or when they've had a failure or two. That's time for you to schedule a session in which you can review with the employee those talents and past successes that have led to your selecting him or her—or that have created the base of confidence that you have in that person.

Your coaching may have to extend beyond a review of strengths and accomplishments to a discussion of those problems or obstacles that the employee may be experiencing. Get the employee's agreement that there is indeed a problem. What you hope to obtain also is a definition of the problem that both of you can agree on. Then encourage the subordinate to develop some solutions with your active help. (See chapter 11 for a fuller discussion of coaching techniques.)

7 *Break the job down into smaller units.* Perhaps the task as a whole looks more formidable than it needs to. Find a way of defining the job in stages or in discrete units. The subordinate might respond by indicating at which stages help will be required—and what kind. By breaking the job into steps, parts, or stages, you can help the subordinate build confidence and a sense of achievement as each step is completed.

8 *Expand the timetable.* If an employee feels the pressure of a deadline, and if it's possible, let the employee know that the schedule is somewhat flexible. "This is the time period I anticipated, but if you think more time is needed, let's discuss it."

Managers need to be alert to the possibility that employees may see the time frame of a task differently. You may have to play an active and continuing role in making sure that deadlines are met. In this case, it is helpful to have intermediate goals to check on progress. If the employee is not following the schedule *you* feel is reasonable (for your purposes), you have to be careful not to communicate your stress if, in actuality, the time available for the job is longer than your preferred schedule. Also, some employees seem unable to gauge the time required. Discreet monitoring by the manager is then in order.

No discussion of a time allocation is complete without reference to the fact that some people need deadlines to do the job. Open-ended schedules for them result in procrastination. Usually with such employees you need to negotiate a deadline that both of you can accept. It's best at the time of negotiation to insist that both of you look at the variables that might hamper progress toward the deadline. Once you agree on the deadline, unless some significant variable occurs that the two of you had not anticipated, insist that the deadline be honored. Problems occur when managers try to play games in setting deadlines. For example, knowing that Martha must have deadline pressure to complete a task, her manager deliberately assigns her a short deadline, extending it later. Martha soon learns that her boss's initial deadline is not the one she need worry about. So she ignores it, frustrating her manager's intentions.

Not an automatic rescuer

One fairly sure way of helping employees to anticipate successful achievement of goals is to be available to bail them out of any difficulties they run into. People will probably be more willing to take on certain duties and assignments if you are known as an automatic rescuer. But the rescuer pays an enormous price. First, if you are busy solving problems for others, you'll find little time to take care of your own.

Also, openness between employees and you will suffer. You want them to be candid with you in how they see their ability to do the work. But if they know that you'll step in at the slightest hint of trouble, they'll have little motivation to level with you.

In time, subordinates' motivation will suffer. Generally, they'll wind up with slight achievements. The credit for the more challenging, troublesome tasks will have to be shared with you.

The important job for the manager is to help an employee develop a higher expectation of achievement in an assignment or a continuing function. The toughest job a manager has is not coming up with answers but knowing what to apply to whom and when; and when to take a more active or passive role; and when to monitor the work overtly—or discreetly.

But then, becoming an expert diagnostician is what makes management of people the endlessly fascinating activity that it is.

9. Creating the right conditions

Imagine, if you will, two divisions of the same organization, both located in the headquarters building.

The work done by the two divisions is somewhat similar. But there the similarity ends. Division A's people are friendly and open. Morale is high. They cooperate freely with one another, although there is a mild competitiveness among them. There is a minimum of supervision—and very little turnover.

Division B, on the other hand, is characterized by poor communication, both from the top down and among department heads. The competitiveness is so fierce that co-workers withhold information from one another. People in one department often know little about what people in other departments are doing. The management is autocratic; the division is highly structured.

It is generally conceded that the route to the top of the corporation is more direct through B than through A. For that reason, I'm sure, a promising young manager in division A was invited by higher management to switch divisions. He turned the offer down, even though he was choosing what seemed to be the slower path upward.

Later, he explained to me, "I've always been ambitious, and I want to get ahead. But I know what it's like over there, and, frankly, I don't think I could have pulled it off. What I'm saying is that I wouldn't have done well under those conditions. Chances are, I'd have blown it."

The climate

The young manager's goal was to be promoted to a higher management position. His transfer to division B was seen as the threshold of the promotion. Yet, he looked at the working conditions that prevailed in that division and concluded he would have problems working effectively. The climate in division B constituted an obstacle.

Work climate—or the environment, as some like to refer to it—can influence the way people feel about what they're doing. It is a situational factor that can add to or detract from the value of the work. It can seem to facilitate the work, or make it look more difficult, as it did for the manager who was invited to change divisions.

Most people, I suspect, would rather work in an atmosphere that is supportive and cooperative, with people contributing to one other, than in one that is combative and highly competitive, with people in conflict and out for only themselves. Most people would choose a work climate that is relaxed and friendly, where they can trust one another, rather than one that is tense, where the people are reticent, suspicious, and uptight.

I discovered this for myself when, as a young man, I experienced a culture shock after I was transferred from a large territory in the West to a smaller metropolitan area in the East. Although the Western region covered four large states, there was almost a community feeling among people in the industry. Much business was done on a highly personal basis. Business relationships sometimes grew like friendships and endured. You became familiar with the competition.

In the East, by contrast, competition was fierce and always changing. Business relationships were based to a great extent on financial considerations. People had less time for socializing. It took a longer time to develop associations with people in the business, to whom a new salesperson was, for a while, just another face.

I knew my business. I had been successful, and I knew that I could be even more successful in my new territory than in the old. But the new climate wasn't to my liking. It wasn't fun. The work lost value. Eventually I resigned.

However, the man who had preceded and the one who succeeded me produced very well under conditions that I disliked. That is an important point to keep in mind. There are highly competitive, very individualistic people for whom challenge is the key factor.

A brilliant young woman with a fresh M.B.A. was offered the opportunity to work in the Atlanta regional office. Interestingly, two of her co-workers had been offered the same position, and they had declined. The problem was the Atlanta regional manager, a hard-driving, demanding, irascible person clearly on the fast track. He was an acknowledged genius. She took the challenge. She felt that if she could work with him, not only could she learn much but she was sure to acquire the reputation of being able to work with even the most difficult people.

In general, however, people prefer to work in a climate that is collaborative, with people supporting one another rather than fighting or undermining them. Since the climate in which the work is to be done affects the value of the work and/or the probability of achievement, managers should move to intervene when excessive conflict between subordinates gets in the way of results. Managers can reduce tension and anxious feelings in employees by making efforts to be more predictable, to apply similar standards to everyone, to reward results, and to discourage behavior that is unreasonably political, competitive, and fragmenting.

Bear in mind that when you assign someone to an atmosphere that is tense, combative, ferociously competitive, and constrictive, you shouldn't be surprised if the employee experiences a reduction in motivation.

Frederick Herzberg would characterize environment as a dissatisfier, not contributing to motivation. But the environment, the situation in which the work is done, is definitely a factor that can enhance or detract from the value of work or can influence the employee's expectation of achievement and success. Thus, the situation surrounding the work, the task, or assignment can affect motivation.

There are at least three other general situational factors: physical environment, geographical location, and personal consideration.

Physical environment

Physical environment is a visible, somewhat obvious factor. To use an extreme example, you delegate to a young assistant the necessary but unglamorous job of cleaning out the files. He has to work for some time in the file room, cramped, with no windows, shut off from the usual contacts with co-workers. It is not a prized assignment, and he shows no enthusiasm. He may work on the files with less than his usual efficiency.

You may find a de-motivating effect when you ask a salesperson to take over an inner city territory. It is old, run-down, dirty, perhaps—in the person's mind—dangerous.

A secretary who has been working in a carpeted space with three others is transferred to a floor-wide, open area in which fifty others work. She feels depressed and works less efficiently than before.

The physical conditions that surround people as they work can affect their perception of the value of the job or their ability to do it successfully. Production managers will tell you that people tend to work better in a plant that is kept orderly and neat, in which housekeeping is strictly enforced. A person who likes a great deal of social contact on the job probably will not be eager to accept a job sitting alone in a room or in a corner with a computer terminal, no matter how much pay is involved. An employee who tends to be claustrophobic will probably feel unable to perform in a small, closed-in space. A person who has been used to privacy might find working in a large, visible area very distracting.

Don't overlook the possibility that the subordinate will relate the physical environment to status. An increase of status can be seen as a reward, making the job more valuable. What is seen as a step down in status can take away from motivation.

It's safe to say that most people would prefer a physical environment that is clean, attractive, and comfortable. In transferring an employee from a surrounding that is less so to one that is more congenial, you can probably anticipate that the person will find the value of the work enhanced or will feel better able to do it. It works the other way, too, as some of the above examples demonstrate.

In short, the physical environment has to be considered in assigning people to jobs and anticipating how they'll perform in them.

Geographical location

As many New York–based corporations have discovered to their dismay, managers no longer necessarily heed the call to the big city. The fact that it is a big city, is expensive, dirty, and that the office is hard to get to and from, can lessen the appeal of the home office, even though that's where the action is supposed to be.

Demographers point out that the Sunbelt states are taking the lead in population growth. And that increase probably isn't due just to retirees. Recently a young man, who had for two years campaigned to become branch manager, was offered the position—in Buffalo. He turned it down. "My wife and I don't like the cold winters," he explained. "I'll wait for something better to come along."

Clearly geographical location affects the value of the work. And it can cause difficulties in the employee's mind as to the chances for successful performance. Going back a few years, I remember that the branch manager sent to replace me in Salt Lake City was terrified of flying. That was a severe handicap in a territory of four large states: Utah, Nevada, Idaho, and Montana, where there was little regular rail service and auto travel between cities consumed precious hours and days. Airplanes in that part of the country were the only practical form of transportation. His effectiveness was seriously hampered by his fear. Clearly he was a poor choice for that kind of territory.

Geographical location is a prime example of how the situation can enhance the value of the work or the probability of being successful. An employee who is devoted to skiing would find living in the American Northeast or mountain West a distinct plus. Similarly, an employee who likes the excitement of a large city would appreciate an assignment to New York, Chicago, or Los Angeles. There are other ways in which management can increase the value of a specific geographical location. For example, in one company three branch offices, located in Chicago, Atlanta, and Dallas, are notably the final field assignments for young potentials. After one of those offices, the next step is a high-level management position in the United States or abroad.

Personal consideration

One Chicago manager told me of a brilliant young subordinate in his department who was, the manager felt, destined to move up fast. The subordinate had spent time in the field, was now in the home office doing a stint in marketing research. Thus, he had practical first-hand field experience and was acquiring the theoretical, planning expertise. "Our Dallas operation was in bad shape. We'd had management turnover, the territories needed restructuring, and our people there were poorly trained in product knowledge," the manager explained. "I offered Cal the opportunity to spend a few months out there getting that operation in shape. It was a situation made to order for him. I knew he could do it. The result would be high visibility for him, both in the field and in the home office."

But Cal turned down the temporary assignment, much to the manager's surprise. After some prodding, Cal explained why. His wife and he were divorcing. Custody of the children had become a big issue. Cal didn't want to be away at that time for an extended period, lest his wife use the absence to argue that he shouldn't have custody.

Personal reasons reduced the value of the assignment. Such reasons can be a cogent factor. Unfortunately, as discussed in chapter 6, it may be the hardest of all the situational factors for the manager to find out. Marital problems, health, anticipation of a job or career change—all can affect the employee's feeling about the task or assignment, or the performance of everyday functions.

The manager's judgment rules here. How much can you ask? How much do you really want to know? (For specific help in this delicate area, you may wish to consult chapter 6.) It may be important, at least, to have the assurance from the employee that the reasons are more personal than job-related, and that, in the case of regular performance that has been slipping, some solution can be found. Counseling may be called for.

Compensating

Sometimes—admittedly—you find it difficult to alter the situation. You can't move the files into a roomy place with lots of windows. Someone has to go to Buffalo or to the inner city. And the unpleasant executive has clout —you can't wish him away. If the situation, the condi-

tions under which the job is to be done, subtracts from
the value of that job or assignment, or causes the employee to suspect that there will be difficulties in doing
it, review what you can do in those two other areas.

VALUE
If the situation detracts from the value, look for ways
to build the value. The manager who wanted a person to
work for the unpleasant, though talented, executive in
Atlanta might have tried to make prospective trans-
ferees aware of the internal, as well as external rewards
possible: "If you prove that you can work with him,
you'll not only come off as a hero to management, but
to yourself. You'll have every right to be confident in
your ability to take on the toughest assignments."

Look at the rewards you have available with which
to recognize special performance. If you don't want to
be, or must not be, specific, you may find it possible at
least to describe in general terms the kinds of rewards
the employee can expect, from money to promotion to
first crack at the next desirable responsibility.

Or this could be the time to get specific. "Look, take
this job (or stick it out) and I promise that I'll put in a
recommendation for a 15 percent increase in pay for you
next year."

In difficult cases, consider giving an immediate reward. One woman, with a newly minted M.B.A. degree,
was asked to take on an important assignment that
meant stepping into the shoes of a manager who was
regarded by subordinates with such fierce loyalty that
a successor was bound to have a rocky time of it. She
was given a special title. In addition to General Manager, which was the predecessor's title, she was made
Assistant Vice-President.

Another value-building approach is to couple the bad
with the better. At a recent conference on productivity,
one organization boasted of its success in getting people
to work in a very monotonous job that had very low

status and appeal. They routinely offered to transfer anyone out of it after four months, at which time boredom usually began to erode the effectiveness of most people. "The Houston branch manager is coming up for retirement next year. Do a good job in Buffalo, and the job in Houston can be yours." Two cautions: one, be sure the subordinate and you agree in advance what a "good job" is, and, two, be thorough in examining the obstacles to his being transferred to Houston before you assure him that it can be done. For example, what will you do if the Chicago branch manager, more senior and experienced (possibly more productive) asks for the Houston spot?

EXPECTANCY

How can you increase the employee's confidence that he or she can successfully do the work? Review the section on probability in the previous chapter, and select those factors that may provide a compensation for the dip in the employee's expectancy.

Perhaps the most important step you can take, if it is possible, is to let the subordinate suggest to you how the task or job can be changed to make it more attractive. You may find that you can make more alterations than you suspected.

No way to improve?

What can you do when you cannot increase the value of the work and there is no need to build up the expectancy of the employee? Don't overlook these options:

1 *Assign a time limit.* One manager put it succinctly when he said after a tough assignment, "They could put me in chains, and I could find a way to tolerate it if I knew for sure I was going to get out—and when." You usually don't have such an extreme assignment, but you can offer a time limit to conditions that are seen

as less than ideal: "Do this for the remainder of the year; then we'll see that you get a new assignment."

2 *Extra support.* You can offer more access to you. "Look, when you're down, call me anytime, just to talk, if you want." This kind of special consideration can help almost any subordinate through a job that, for some reason or other, has become less valuable or more difficult.

3 *Make a special plea.* Sometimes it may come down to this: "Lorraine, this job is very important to me. I'm asking you to do this, even though I know it's not the kind of work you get excited about. Believe me, I won't forget that you've done me a favor." Making an occasional, personal plea or request for a favor is perfectly in line.

While it's true that the situation surrounding the doing can detract from its motivational value, it's also true, as I've pointed out, that situational factors may, for some, enhance motivation. You may have to look harder, but the chance is that someone will respond favorably to what others would regard as adverse circumstances.

10: Making appraisals work

If you don't know where you're going, according to the old saying, any road will do. Similarly, if you don't know how well you're doing, how will you know when you've done it? If you want employees to do a good job for you, you need to tell them how well they are doing what you expect them to do. You need to give them feedback. Unfortunately, what I often hear from subordinates—managers as well as rank-and-file—is the complaint, "I know when I've goofed, but I never hear when I'm doing well."

Some managers seem to lean toward negative feedback. I suspect their rationale is that employees should know when they're performing well. The manager is there to call attention to any deviation. Unfortunately, any manager who gives only negative feedback can earn the title of "bad news Charlie." That is perhaps the least unkind thing that can be said. In one organization a particular manager's performance appraisals are referred to by subordinates as "grudge time." Once or twice a year this manager unloads his laundry list of complaints and feelings on hapless subordinates.

Employees should look forward to appraisals as information time. It is "How-am-I-doing?" time. It may be an occasion for reassurance: "You're doing well." Preferably, appraisals also answer the question, "How can I do better?"

Many managers are uncomfortable with the performance appraisal function of their jobs. Either through inadequate training or as a result of their organization's evaluation system, they feel as if they are sitting in judgment, rather like a teacher grading pupils. Needless to say, employees who are being appraised feel much the same, as pupils being graded. It is a serious misuse of an essential management function.

Performance appraisals constitute just one phase of an effective feedback program. Other components are coaching, counseling, and on-the-spot informal reinforcement or criticism. Each one has its own purpose, even when they are combined, and each one will be considered individually in this book. Ideally, they should be considered separate functions. Most managers, most of the time, do some of them. Some managers, some of the time, do all of them. All managers should perform all four functions in a conscientious, consistent, systematic manner.

If they don't regularly appraise, coach, counsel, criticize, and reinforce, they run the danger of not meeting their own or their subordinates' needs. Without feedback, both managers and subordinates operate, to some extent, blindly and by chance.

The feedback transaction

Good feedback goes both ways. Managers need information from employees. They need to know how employees see their tasks—difficult, too easy, unnecessarily complicated, without purpose, etc. A feedback system provides controls that show what is, or is not, going according to plan. The information helps measure progress toward the goals that were set earlier. What may emerge is an awareness that the plan is not workable, that those goals need changing.

A good feedback system has the benefit of uncovering problems and obstacles. It provides opportunities for managers and subordinates to find solutions to the problems that prevent them from working well. Interestingly, there are times when subordinates know more about a problem, and can come up with more solutions, than their managers.

There is also a long-range payoff for the manager who regularly and conscientiously schedules feedback sessions. For one thing, the manager confirms his or her dedication to good performance. The manager wants results—for himself or herself, for the organization, for the employees themselves. Appraisals, coaching, counseling, criticism, and reinforcement say to subordinates, "You see, I mean what I say when I talk about the effectiveness of everyone in the department."

It is through feedback, especially coaching, that managers come to know better just what resources they have to work with in their subordinates. You have to assume that, no matter how long you have worked with an individual, there are still things you don't know about that person. There are probably aspects of that person that he or she doesn't know about, or knows dimly. It is a learning opportunity for both of you.

Thus, any feedback is a transaction. You approach it as you would any transaction, asking questions such as these: "What do I want to happen as a result of this session?"; "What do I think the employee wants as a result of this session?"; "How can we both get some, or all, of what we want?"

Another way of describing the transaction is to say that the manager is Assertive-Responsive. It's not enough to make your needs known. You have also to recognize that the other person is bringing needs to the discussion, has interests, can provide certain resources and strength to help make the transaction work—for everyone's benefit. And that can only happen if the manager talks *and* listens.

Appraisal systems

Is your appraisal system working for you? Does it tell you which subordinates are performing well and which are not? Does it reveal weaknesses in your goal setting and work assignments? Do your appraisals provide reasonably objective indicators of where and with whom you should invest the major part of your time and energy to get the best results, the most improvement? Can you estimate, from your evaluations, what kind of performance you can expect in the next, say, six months?

Many managers would have difficulty answering *yes* to these questions. Their appraisal systems do not provide workable data. In fact, some of the most elaborate and carefully constructed appraisal systems produce much information that is useless. For example, some appraisals require managers to estimate the potential of their subordinates, to hazard a guess—that's what it is —as to what grade in the organization an employee might be able to reach. How does a manager deal with such a complex task? Many don't try. One manager told me that he routinely replies that all of his subordinates are qualified to be president of the corporation.

Other appraisal forms require supervisors to evaluate personality characteristics, traits, and attitudes. It's another guessing game. Managers are asked to rate what they cannot see, to measure what defies measurement, or to judge factors that may have little to do with performance. Would you know how to evaluate the degree of maturity of an employee? I'm not sure how I would define it. One manager put it wisely when he declared in a workshop, "I don't give a hang about a person's attitude. It's behavior I want. The employee's behavior is my business; his personality is his."

What are some of the characteristics of a good approach to performance appraisal?

Effective appraisals

The effective performance appraisal has at least two steps, written and verbal. First, the appraising manager puts in writing an evaluation of the subordinate who is being appraised. Then the appraiser meets with the appraised to discuss what has been written.

The evaluation process should take place at least once a year, although many organizations find it desirable to require it two, three, and even four times in twelve months. Appraisal times should be scheduled so that employees come to know when they'll occur. When they are not scheduled, there is a temptation for the appraiser to act on impulse instead of to prepare carefully. For example, a supervisor might be annoyed with an employee and decide that this is as good a time as ever to do some appraising. Even when that is not the case, the employee may be apprehensive and distracted, wondering why the session was called at that time, if the manager might have an ulterior motive.

Both employee and manager should have ample time to get their thoughts and papers together for a constructive appraisal session.

A good appraisal program should also follow some logical guidelines:

1 *The appraisal program should confine itself as much as possible to work-related criteria.* Typical examples of job-related measures are the amount of work performed, whether deadlines are met, the quality and accuracy of work performed. Some appraisals are tied to goals and their achievement. For example, goal A was achieved totally; goal B was 88 percent achieved, etc. An appraisal might include measures of improvement in quantity and quality of work since previous evaluation periods.

Having to rate overall performance—for example, assigning a rating of 85 percent to a subordinate's efforts—causes many managers great frustration. The use of percentages in evaluating effectiveness of performance does not lessen the arbitrariness of that method. How does a manager distinguish between a rating of 80 percent and 85 percent unless the figures show what proportion of the expected work was done satisfactorily? Estimating performance effectiveness comes uncomfortably close, for many, to the teacher deciding between a B+ and A−.

An effective appraisal minimizes reliance on general traits or personal characteristics. Measuring enthusiasm, initiative, and commitment is precarious. It is, as I suggested, hard to relate them to an employee's performance.

2 *The program must be applied uniformly.* Organizations that use multiple appraisal systems, or different systems for management and rank-and-file employees, should be careful that all employees within a given group are evaluated by the same system. When they are evaluated according to different tests, forms, and procedures, the variances in individual employees' evaluations may depend more on the system used than on work performance. Moreover, it would be unfair, and perhaps discriminatory, to compare one employee's performance with another's when employees have not been appraised using the same criteria. I oppose informal appraisals, without written instruments or guidelines. To leave the criteria and timing up to the appraiser is to invite legal problems and seriously undermine the reliability of the appraisal.

The amount of training that appraisers receive is an important factor in how accurate, consistent, and reliable the evaluations are.

3 *Finally, the effective appraisal program should work.* An evaluation system must operate smoothly to yield the best results. The system should not be overly complex for managers to understand and implement, nor should it take too much of a manager's time. Appraisal forms should be simple, short, and, in general, easy to fill out. Appraisers should be fully familiar with procedures. They should know, for example, whom they are to evaluate, how often the appraisal is to be conducted, who is to review the appraisals, when interviews with employees are to be scheduled, what the proper procedures are for handling complaints from employees. Furthermore, the procedure must carry out its objectives. This is the key test. If the evaluation procedure does not meet the objectives mapped out for it when it was put into operation, then something is wrong, and review is in order.

Reducing the bias

No matter how well a system is designed, the people running it, in this case managers and supervisors who conduct the appraisals, are subject to shortcomings. For example:

1 *Halo effect.* Raters may allow one characteristic of an employee to have an excessive influence on their rating of all other factors. The quality may be one that the appraiser dislikes, though usually that characteristic is one that the appraiser admires, for example, competitiveness or aggressiveness, precision or deliberativeness, deference to authority, and so on.

Sam is loyal, a quality that his boss admires. He has been working in the same department for twenty-eight years, does what he is told, never questions. Sam's work is mediocre, but he always gets great evaluations.

2 *Leniency and strictness.* Some supervisors tend to be overly generous in their ratings; they give unwarranted high marks, often out of fear that they will make a mistake by being too harsh. Some supervisors go to the other extreme: They tend to rate employees unnecessarily harshly. Excessive leniency or strictness generally stems from the differing personal standards that individual supervisors have. Department-to-depart-

ment ratings that vary from extremely high to extremely low can seriously impair an appraisal program.

3 *Averaging.* Some raters like to "play it safe." They avoid placing employees at the extreme ends of the scale—either high or low—but consistently give employees average ratings. That way they feel they can avoid making errors in judgment and being unfair to anyone. Averaging may also be attributable to the supervisor's own standards, against which most employees may be just average performers. In other cases, supervisors do an inadequate job of observing how individual employees are performing. So when appraisal time arrives, they do not really know whether employees have done well or not. Best, they reason, to give them all average scores.

4 *Personal bias.* This is related to the halo effect except that it involves more general feelings of liking or disliking. Most people have seen personal bias at work. One of the extreme examples I've seen involved a woman whose productivity was consistently low. She usually came to work a half-hour later than other employees, and left that much earlier. Her absentee rate was the highest in the department. Other employees gnashed their teeth in frustration, if not in anger. But the woman's supervisor never criticized her, although she did take others to task for trying the same behavior. Whenever the supervisor spoke of the erring employee, it was always sympathetically or admiringly. "You know, her health is quite fragile," or, "Oh, she's such a pro. It was a lucky day when she joined us." The reason for the good fortune was, I'm told, not apparent to other employees, who found they had to work harder because of this woman's underproduction. Evidently the supervisor found something to like in the subordinate.

How to make appraisals work

1 *Use goals.* Where possible, combine appraisal with a goal-setting program. Employees are less likely to question evaluations based on goals they have agreed to. And appraisers are less likely to get in the way of their appraisals when they are reporting on the achievement of specified objectives.

2 *Let the employee contribute.* Some organizations require that a completed appraisal form be shown to each appraised employee, who then signs it. But what if the employee disagrees with portions? One answer is to permit the employee to submit in writing any variance and to file that dissent with the evaluation. What I find especially intriguing are the systems that ask employees to appraise themselves as well as having a supervisor or manager evaluate them. Then the two meet to compare evaluations.

3 *Require that appraisals be explained.* Instruct appraisers to explain the reasons for their appraisals to employees during feedback sessions. Also, appraisers should document for the files why they recommend merit increases, promotions, demotions, or dismissals.

However, that does not necessarily mean that the documentation should be part of the appraisal interview itself. Many management experts say that the only reward that should be extended during appraisals is praise. Their reasoning is that, if employees know that pay raises or other rewards are announced at appraisal time, they may not hear other things that their managers want them to hear. Proponents of the method that combines the appraisal discussion with giving rewards argue that it emphasizes that rewards are determined by performance. A compromise, it seems to me, would be to establish clearly that appraisal is for evaluating performance thus far and setting new goals. Rewards, based on that performance, are announced a few days later.

4 *Have appraisals reviewed.* Each appraiser should have his or her appraisals reviewed by the next level manager. Even if the higher manager doesn't know the appraised employees well, he or she will be able to note patterns in the appraiser's evaluations that could signal bias, for example, repeated strong emphasis on certain points, characteristics, or behaviors, to the exclusion of or with a de-emphasis on others. Labels are tell-tale. I knew one manager who frequently characterized a subordinate as "negative." It almost goes without saying that he was not effective with the subordinate. A review of his appraisals would have picked this up.

One radical proposal—at least I'm sure that many would consider it so—suggests that employees evaluate their appraisers on their skills at appraising subordinates. A number of low ratings would surely alert the appraiser's boss that something was going wrong. But evaluation of the boss would, in most organizations, have to be made by subordinates in a confidential form directly to their boss's manager, to become part of their boss's performance appraisal. That is, if any significant, honest data were to be developed. Employees would probably worry about a reprisal if their boss were to see their evaluations.

Predictable appraisals

Ideally, what goes on during an appraisal should be predictable. It seems to me that an employee should have a fair idea of what the supervisor is going to say, especially if the evaluation involves goals that have been set previously. When standards and objectives are clear, when appraisals are regular, when criteria are performance-related, there should be little mystery about what is to take place. Except in the case of a relatively new employee, appraisal feedback sessions shouldn't produce major surprises.

Thus, except in the case of failing performance, the appraisal process should produce no more than minimal stress. In fact, employees who are performing well might even look forward to evaluation as confirmation of their own opinions of their work. The chance to talk about the near future, even to set interesting new goals, is appealing—or should be.

However, the good feelings in both appraiser and appraised should not encourage them to overlook or "forgive" expectations or objectives that have not been met. Underachievement of agreed-upon goals could be an indicator of trouble, either in the employee or in the goals themselves.

Should counseling or coaching be part of the appraisal discussion? Sometimes, but the appraisal process is chiefly concerned with what has taken place in the recent past, say three to six months, and what it is hoped will happen during the next appraisal period, again, perhaps three to six months. Appraisals therefore concentrate on the here-and-now. *Now* usually covers a maximum period of one year—past, present, and future.

The *here* constraint is equally important. The appraiser is evaluating what the appraised can apply to the job now. What are discussed are the employee's actual talents, skills, and knowledge. Problems that affect performance may call for coaching or counseling, and if so, the manager may choose to include one of those functions with the appraisal.

There are no hard and fast rules. My bias leads me to recommend that the manager keep the appraisal clear and clean: "This is what we agreed that you would do, and this is what you have done." If there is a shortfall, then go into the reasons. Were the goals unrealistic? Is there an obstacle, from outside or within the employee?

Is the obstacle one-time or continuing? What can we do about it? Finally, let's talk about your goals for the next period.

Coaching or counseling may be indicated. But to the extent possible, keep them apart. They have their own purposes, as we'll see.

11: Coaching for growth

Would you have any problem agreeing with this statement: Your primary concern is the effectiveness of your subordinates in carrying out your organizational goals? As a manager, you could hardly disagree. Here's another statement: Coaching employees is necessary to achieve and maintain both personal and organizational effectiveness. Again you would agree. Do you coach as much as you should? If you are like most managers, you would have to answer no.

If you're not convinced that you belong with the majority, consider the following questions:

Recall the contacts that you've had with each of your subordinates during the past month. Did you try to take advantage of every chance to teach the subordinate, to provide some kind of learning opportunity?

Do you have a regular schedule for discussing with subordinates those skills and talents that can be developed for the future? Do you conscientiously try to maintain that schedule?

Do you have in mind for each subordinate one or two experiences or assignments that could stretch the subordinate, contribute to his or her growth and development?

Have you provided one or two such developmental experiences for each subordinate during the past six months?

Do you have some mutually agreed-upon plan of action for the growth and development of each of your subordinates, either on the present job or for some future responsibilities?

Few managers would answer affirmatively to all the questions and pass the test. Probably it's because the terms *growth* and *development* carry a long-term connotation. They point to the future. Meanwhile, here is today with all of its problems and pressures. Everyone thinks, "What can be put off until tomorrow?" Of course. But there are immediate needs for coaching— and immediate rewards.

Coaching for today

While the appraisal is a formal step, usually scheduled and at fixed times of the year, coaching takes place in the interim and is informal. Coaching an employee deepens and broadens the communication channel. Coaching enables a manager to add to an employee's knowledge and to sharpen certain skills. Through coaching the manager helps the subordinates to find a solution to a problem or a new and better way to perform a task or function. This kind of coaching may be initiated by the employee who recognizes a need for help, or by the manager who spots a need to intervene.

Salespeople in particular are accustomed to this kind of informal, impromptu discussion with their managers. It's often referred to as *curbstone coaching.* After the manager and the salesperson have made a call on a prospect, they sit in the car or over coffee to analyze the interview. If the call was successful, the two will examine the relative strength of the tactics that the salesperson used during the presentation. If no order resulted, they will try to isolate the reason why the interview didn't work.

Some problems are more complicated and far-reaching. For example, Mike, a supervisor, asks for some time with his boss, Art, to talk about some problem Mike has been having with Bill, one of his subordinates. Bill has been in the department for about twelve years. Mike is relatively new as a supervisor, having been promoted about a year previously.

Mike: Bill is a real problem. He's turning out less and less work. Many times what he does has to be returned for redoing.

Art: What do you mean "many times"?

Mike: I've been keeping track. About one out of four jobs goes back.

Art: You've spoken to him about it?

Mike: Yes. He seemed quite surprised to hear that his work was below par. He said, "I thought I was doing okay."

Art: Let's see the records you've been keeping. Hmmm. What did he say when you showed him these?

Mike: He said that he's been doing the cost reports the same way he did them while Frank was his supervisor, and that Frank never complained, and he doesn't know why I make things so tough on him.

Art: Is it true that he's doing everything as he always did?

Observation: There are two mistakes Art has made with this question. First, it asks for a yes or no answer. That kind of a question seldom conveys much usable information, especially if the purpose is to encourage the other person to volunteer information. The second problem is that the question calls for a judgment that may masquerade as objective. True, boss-subordinate communications don't have to abide by the law of evidence, but both people have to recognize that there are considerably more subjective than objective data. A better alternative is:

Art: What's your feeling about his answer?

Mike: Well, I realize that he and Frank worked

together a long time, and they had a good friendship. I came along and took over from Frank. I suspect that Bill resents that. In fact, I'd go so far as to say I think Bill thought he'd get Frank's job.

Art: Well, could be. What do you recommend be done about the performance?

Observation: Many problem-solving discussions spend too much time analyzing the reasons for the problem. Most people like occasionally to play detective or psychiatrist. However, Art, while not discounting Mike's analysis, quite properly directs Mike's attention to what alternatives he wants.

Mike: I could tell Bill that he's not working for Frank any longer, and that he has to learn to do the work according to my standards.

Art: That is an option. What will you do if he just goes along as he has been?

Mike: Fire him.

Art: Well, that is another resort. A last resort. Let's look at some other options.

Observation: Art is wisely avoiding an either-or approach to a solution. Most people, especially in a severe problem situation, do not take time to consider how many options they really have. Art encourages Mike to look at alternative solutions.

Art: If you could get Bill to meet your standards, how would you feel about his staying on?

Mike: I'd be happy to have him stay. I'm not out to get rid of him.

Art: Then what do you think the first step is?

Mike: I suppose I ought to sit down with Bill and tell him what I expect from him from now on. That's probably something I should have done a long time ago. But Bill's been here so long, I guess I always took it for granted that he knew what to do.

Art: He *did* know what to do—as far as Frank was concerned. Now he needs to know what you expect.

Okay, I suggest that you and I meet again after Bill and you agree that he can do what you expect.

Art has tentatively agreed on the standards Mike believes his subordinate, Bill, can meet. Mike now needs Bill's acceptance of those standards. Only then will all three of them know how and when they will be able to judge results. Later, after Mike and Bill have talked, Mike reports back to his boss.

Art: Do you anticipate any obstacles? Do you believe Bill is going to have problems meeting these objectives?

Mike: I think that in certain areas he needs some refresher training. Some of the others in the section have developed better work methods.

Art: What would happen if one of the others tutored Bill?

Mike: Well, he has more overall knowledge than most. He would probably resent being tutored.

Art: What would you think about setting up a brief seminar where everyone could exchange information?

Mike: You know, that's interesting. Bill has an awful lot of stuff stored in his head. Maybe he might open up.

Art: All right. What I'm hearing is that you think he can teach them from his experience, and they can help him to be more efficient—if he accepts.

Mike: I think that's probably right. Everyone would benefit.

Art: And that approach would lessen the threat to Bill.

If Mike reflects on the interviews with his boss, Art, he'll realize that not only has Art helped him to work out an immediate problem, but he has given Mike some pointers in solving problems in general.

A coaching sequence

In problem-centered coaching, you may find it helpful to follow these steps:

1 Whether the subordinate initiates the interview or you do, get agreement that a problem exists. You may well have your own opinion on the nature of the problem and how it developed. And you may assume that the other person sees the problem from your perspective. That may not be necessarily true.

A good way to approach the definition of the problem is to describe how it manifests itself. Use observed behavior: "She is at least twenty minutes late two or three times a week." Performance records provide objective data: "That unit's output has dropped 18 percent in three months, and they've had no change of personnel." There are other kinds of documentation: "XYZ Company has 35 percent of the market, and we can't seem to gain more than 20 percent."

Don't rush to a solution. Nor is it a good idea to *insist*, as some managers do, that employees come to you with a solution as well as a problem. For one thing, you may discourage them from letting you know that some problems exist (for which they can't come up with solutions). For another, they may define the problem in a way (not necessarily accurately) that facilitates an answer. In other words, they may alter the problem to fit the solution.

2 Define the various options. This problem that you've agreed on obviously needs to be corrected. But what kind of situations would you both prefer to see in its stead? Asking the question this way may open up new possibilities that otherwise would not have been considered. After all, correcting a problem may result in no more than bringing you back from a deviation that has occurred—bringing you back to where you were. Thinking of alternatives may advance you beyond where you were.

I should acknowledge at this point in the book, I frequently advise you to look for solutions or alternatives rather than causes. I am not saying that people should never look for causes. But very often, seeking causes is equated with, "Who's to blame for this?" Developing alternatives avoids the game of pin-the-tail-on-the-donkey. When people suspect that the manager may be interested in fixing blame—perhaps even more so than finding a solution—they often close up, keeping vital information to themselves.

3 Set goals and subgoals that will help you to know when you're making progress. You need some standards and measurements. Progress can be measured in a behavior change (better telephone technique that results in fewer complaints from callers), units of output (15 percent more per day), new competence (the ability to sell a different product or program for the first time). Remember that goals are set in a time frame, so establish time limits as well.

For the most part, Art and Mike followed these first three steps. Some of the additional recommendations might also serve you:

4 Have a plan B. Retain some or at least one of the original options that you considered. Your original selection, no matter how well intentioned and thought out, may have to be scrapped or modified. Furthermore, you as the manager may have to intervene if your subordinate's efforts prove faulty. The situation may be too risky for you to sit back and wait for the subordinate to recognize the fact.

5 Determine your role. Should you provide authority, training, reassignment? What counseling and feedback may be desirable? If the problem is one that a subordinate has in managing another worker, get the supervisor's agreement as to what part you should play.

6 Set up a program of review. Once you've determined a plan of action, you have to review it from time to time to make sure it's working. It's best to establish a schedule of review in advance so that no one forgets it should be done—and so that no one thinks you're meddling.

7 Give feedback. If the plan isn't followed because, in your view, the subordinate isn't following the game plan, let it be known. If the subordinate is succeeding, it's extremely important to let him or her know.

Is short-term coaching restricted to problems? Of course not. A supervisor may come to you with an idea or a plan: "I would like to introduce job rotation into my department so that employees can cover for each other." Or a manager may present you with a decision: "I need a supervisor to head up the delinquent accounts section. I have three people who might be qualified. How do I know which one is most suitable?" Such requests usually deserve some coaching by you. Many of the steps described above can be altered to fit planning or decision-making coaching. Your role, as in problem-centered interviews, is to help your subordinates to define both the situation and the options, to evaluate the options, and in some cases to set goals. You must also decide on your role, and if review is desirable, give feedback.

Coaching for growth

A long-term coaching process is usually initiated by the manager to help employees to develop their resources. It is directional, growth-centered rather than problem-oriented.

It's the long-term coaching that managers usually have to remind themselves to do. When there is no problem demanding immediate attention, there are nevertheless human resources that need development. There are employees who are hungry for guidance and feedback, who want to be assured that management is concerned about their future and value. They seek advice, learning opportunities, information about what the organization can offer. Thus, the manager who wants to increase the value and effectiveness of his or her work group, who would like to be known as a developer of talent, who seeks to increase the motivational forces within subordinates, cannot afford to bypass this coaching responsibility.

Whereas appraisals work with what is already available, coaching for growth deals with what is potentially there. But you may have to look for the potential. For example, here is an informal coaching session between Mark and his boss Phyllis.

Phyllis: Mark, I have my own view of how you do your job, but I'd like to get a better idea of how you *see* your job. What do you like about it? What do you think you do best? Maybe we can compare notes.

Mark: How I see it?

Phyllis: Maybe I ought to back up. How do you feel you perform in your job?

Mark: Pretty well. I don't really have any problem.

Phyllis: But there are perhaps some things you'd like to do more of.

Mark: I like talking with customers on the telephone. And I'm doing a lot of that. But what I think would be more enjoyable is to be able to talk with the same customers—

Phyllis: Instead of taking whatever call is coming in if you're the processor available.

Mark: Yes, and what I'm saying is that the job—I think—would be more satisfying if each of us had our own bloc of customers. That way we could get to know them better.

Phyllis: That's very interesting. What kinds of advantages do you think that kind of system would have over how we're doing it now?

Mark: Well, for one thing, it would make the job a little more personal. Right now we pick up the phone and take any call from anyone anywhere in the United States. It would be a lot more fun to be able to say, "Hi, Mr. Johnson. Good to talk to you. Did you get your shipment last week okay?" That sort of thing.

Phyllis: I see what you mean. It sounds very interesting. Let me ask you this question: Suppose Mr. Johnson called while you were tied up. How would he feel about waiting?

Mark: I thought about that. One thing the operator could say, "Mark's on the phone. May I have him call you back as soon as he's off?"

Phyllis: That might work. On the other hand, Mr. Johnson may say, "I can't wait. I want to get this order in the works. I have to get out of here for an appointment."

Mark: Hmmm. Well, here's another way we might try. If Mr. Johnson doesn't want to wait, we let him talk to another processor—whoever's available. Then, later, I call him back on the WATS line and say, "Sorry I wasn't available, Mr. Johnson. I just called to make sure everything was handled the way you wanted it. By the way, I notice that you've been ordering in biweekly lots the last couple of times. You know, there's a way you could take advantage of a 5 percent discount if you placed two orders at once. The volume would qualify."

Phyllis: This is all fascinating. I think we need to know more about how it might work. Would you be willing to sketch it out on paper, how you think we could get it to work? And while you're doing it, make two lists—one to spell out the advantages over the present system, the other to cover possible disadvantages.

Mark consents—probably enthusiastically. For Phyllis, the manager, this is a potentially rewarding session. But it is only a beginning, even though she has uncovered or reinforced important knowledge. Essentially, Mark seems to like what he is doing. He thinks it can be done in a way that is more interesting for the processors and customers, as well as more profitable for the company, because Mark is thinking not only as a processor but as a salesman. Phyllis would be justified if she suspected that Mark has some managerial ability. He is thinking as a manager would.

Phyllis has already made the step to the next coaching session. Mark has agreed to draw up a proposal. Undoubtedly Phyllis will have to help him in shaping it. If it seems workable, she might suggest a test. That would provide another opportunity for her to learn more about Mark's potential. She might ask him to draw up suggestions for training processors in the new system, for working with the data processing people to develop the necessary programming, and so forth.

Obviously, the important point is: Coaching is a continuing process. Each session provides you with data with which you can plan future coaching.

There are any number of questions that can lead to the information that Phyllis uncovered. You might wish to refer back to chapter 6 for general questions that you'll find useful in the coaching process.

Specific situations can trigger coaching. For example:

Observed behavior. "I gather that Mr. McCarthy was irate when he called in. Yet you managed to calm him down and save the order. You seem to like contact with customers. You also seem to work very well under pressure." Where might these skills lead?

The record. "You stepped in when Jack became ill, and not only did you keep the operation going, but you actually increased output by more than 20 percent by rearranging the group." What does this accomplishment suggest?

Definable strengths. "Time after time, whenever there

was an argument on a potential conflict in meetings,
I've seen you step in and defuse the situation. Not
only that, but people leave feeling good." How can this
talent be put to general use?

Reports. "People I've talked to say they find you easy
to work with. Not only do you have a good sense of
humor, but you are generally positive." What is the
significance of this asset?

A caution: However well meaning your questions
are, you have to consider the possibility that they can
seem threatening to the subordinate. You'll be fortunate indeed if you can begin an effective coaching process with a relatively new employee. There must be time
for a sufficient trust to be developed. Subordinates must
see that you really are concerned about their growth
and development. They must be assured through your
behavior that you won't ridicule them should they happen to reveal ambitions that are deep and heretofore
unrevealed.

Once you uncover a potential skill, work to find out
whether there is interest in developing it. You may have
to spur the interest by describing the various situations
in which the skill or predilection can be applied usefully
—a positive function, task, etc. Is there sufficient interest to pursue it? If there is, what can be done to develop
it? Should you suggest training, a program of education, reading, consultation with experts, an assignment?

Don't commit yourself to a course of action without
first making sure that the employee is serious about it,
too.

In coaching, whether you start with general areas of
strength, or with specific questions that are designed to
elicit information on observed or reported behavior or
on accomplishments, be sure that the session ends specifically—what is to be done, how is it to be done, in what
time period, etc.

One general recommendation that I would make is
to try to avoid coming across as a psychologist. People

tend to get nervous if they think you are defining them in psychological terms. Avoid the jargon. I once had forceful evidence of this when I considered putting out a memo to professional members on my staff suggesting that each of them talk with me about how they could create more space for themselves—direction, freedom, work enrichment. I think I also acknowledged that I was aware that they—most of them, anyway—wanted to "push out their boundaries." One of my colleagues—wisely, I believe—discouraged me from distributing my memo. "You're going to threaten some of these people terribly," he said. I think he was right. So I've since tried to avoid getting into a psychological posture when talking with people who work with me.

Giving them what they need to know

Coaching is necessary for you if you are dedicated to developing the resources you have available. And you can't really do an effective job of planning for the future until you have a clear idea of the actual and potential talent in your work group to meet the needs of the future. Coaching encourages a sense of collaboration: We're both going for the same things; we're both going to win if we work together.

Collaboration needs openness between those involved in the working relationship. Thus, a coaching session provides you with the chance to bring the employee up to date on changes that could affect his or her future. For example, these potential obstacles or opportunities:

> *Organizational changes.* What departments or divisions are to be phased out or merged? What new managerial or professional positions are being contemplated?

> *Staffing changes.* What internal expansions or cutbacks are being considered?

Budget changes. What monies are being included for the first time or are being increased or reduced? There might be a greater allowance, for instance, for management development or tuition refund.

New facilities. The construction of a plant or laboratory or branch might offer significant opportunities for advancement.

New projects or plans. The launching of a new product line, to cite one example, could open doors.

The above are some of the significant developments in the offing that could be opportunities for career advancement. Even if, because of confidentiality, you can't be specific about the developments, you can at least give some advice as to how the employee can best prepare, what skills or knowledge would be helpful. One result of your coaching, you hope, will be the encouragement of subordinates to do their own assignments, to study the opportunities, to gauge their own talents in terms of the organization's needs, to develop a growth mentality that will discourage obsolescence.

But there can be another result of your extensive coaching of especially important employees. The coaching can be perceived as a reward for good performance and for the continuing actualization of potential skills. The employee says, "The boss is willing to take the time, because I am worth it."

12: Counseling for change

A salesperson fails to make the required number of calls on prospects week after week. An engineer fails to meet deadlines for completion and submission of technical reports. A supervisor creates conflicts that make it difficult to work with other supervisors.

Wanted: a change of behavior. As manager, you want the calls made, the deadlines met, cooperation extended. It's time for a counseling session. Employees with performance problems should receive counseling when the need becomes apparent—when that performance drops, standards are not met, goals are not achieved. Of course, anyone can have an off week. You don't rush to counsel a subordinate because there's a slight or temporary deviation from the norm you have established. But when it becomes apparent that the performance problem may persist, and that, if it does, the subordinate's productivity (and that of others) will suffer significantly, something has to be done—quickly.

Counseling is usually a moderate to high stress situation—for both the manager and subordinate. When necessary counseling is delayed, that delay often results in more stress. One manager decided that she could no longer hold off on talking to a bright, talented young subordinate who was falling seriously short of agreed-upon objectives. She had delayed, hoping that the problem would correct itself. When she opened the subject with the employee, he said, "I've been wondering when you were going to talk to me about it." He had been expecting—even, as it turned out, wanting—the session. He knew he was in trouble, but he didn't know how to ask for help.

That situation illustrates an important point: No one *wants* to be ineffective. There may be a difference in the way the manager and subordinate define effective. But it is hard to believe that an employee wishes to be incompetent or inadequate (except in the infrequent case in which an employee rebels against a manager and decides on a policy of noncooperation). Most people can change—and will change if it makes sense to them. They want to grow, to become more effective. Just because they don't ask for help, that doesn't indicate that they don't want it.

Thus, it is especially important that, during counseling, the manager approach the employee with the "you're OK" message. Take a pointer from the church: Hate the sin but love the sinner. For the most part, managers don't have to deal with sin. The parallel is this: "You're OK but some of your behavior isn't." The principle is that people will respond to positive expectations. The manager approaches counseling with the attitude, "I want you to be effective, and I know you want to be effective. Let's see how we can achieve that." It is necessary that you believe others want to grow just as you want to grow and want them to grow.

When managers approach counseling negatively or pessimistically, when they reveal even the slightest trace that they doubt whether this will work, but are simply going through the motions, they risk a self-fulfilling prophecy. Employees pick up the negative vibrations. They may agree: "What's the use?"

The question frequently arises, "Is the performance appraisal discussion a good time for counseling?" If that's when the problem becomes clear, and the data support the evidence, then the answer may be yes. But I do have a reservation: Combining a performance appraisal session with counseling the subordinate on a problem can be cumbersome. A lot of territory has to be covered, and much time consumed. Not only could the prolonged interview create an overload for the subordinate, it could serve you poorly by blunting the impact of some of your key points. It's possible that you will be trying to get across too many messages at once. The high stress related to counseling may get in the way of a satisfactory performance appraisal discussion.

Counseling skills

For the manager, there are some other facts about counseling to keep in mind:

1 *The person being counseled usually will react negatively before reacting positively.* The reason is that the subordinate is under stress and probably defensive. Even though you are optimistic about a change of behavior, even though you believe the employee is willing to make it, expect an immediate negative response. Allow for it. Be accepting when you see the negative, defensive behavior. You can empathize with the employee who is under the stress of criticism.

Sometimes the negative feelings don't immediately come out. I recall once when an employee who was usually quite volatile went through a counseling session with me very calmly, listening and agreeing. It just wasn't his usual behavior. Sure enough, the next morning he strode into my office, closed the door, and said in a tense voice, "All right, let's talk." Then I observed the response that I had expected the day before. Everything worked out fine; it just took longer. The manager who is not prepared for a negative stressful reaction may respond in kind, which often means an end to any possibility of a constructive exchange.

2 *In counseling, two types of listening are required.* There are things that are said, and there are the things that are not said. The employee may not volun-

teer all the necessary information. (Indeed, the subordinate may not have a clear idea of what the problem is.) For example, the salesman who is not making enough calls complains that he has to spend too much time servicing his customers. What does he mean by that? Is he selling carelessly so that he has to soothe disgruntled customers? Is he inventing reasons for making service calls on customers rather than sales visits to prospects? Or is there a breakdown in the quality of the product that should be looked into?

Sometimes the subordinate will assure you that the counseling session has gone well, everything is fine, changes will be made. Such external acceptance, however, is questionable when the employee is obviously trying to keep hands from trembling. Or when the smile is forced. Something clearly is not being said.

3 *The manager should be understanding without losing sight of objectives.* That goes both ways, of course. Managers can't afford to get so locked in to the change they want that they lose understanding of their employee's plight. In a counseling session you may hear any number of sad stories. Some of them may be rationalizations, some not. But you don't want to lose sight of the fact that the employee probably takes them very seriously. There is nothing contradictory in the manager's saying, "Yes, I can understand how you feel," or "I agree that you've certainly felt as if you were under a lot of pressure" while insisting that reasonable objectives and standards be met.

There is always the possibility that you may discover that those objectives are not so reasonable, after all.

4 *Counseling is a learning opportunity—for both manager and subordinate.* The subordinate learns what needs to be done and how. And so does the manager. Counseling sessions are not punitive; they are characterized by understanding as well as firmness. Openness is vital. But the chances of achieving openness are slim unless the manager can convince subordinates that he or she is really interested in their well-being as well as that of the department. Counseling often provides the manager with insights into how employees see their well-being, how they feel about what they are or are not doing. There should be, therefore, a lot of communication back and forth. And if the manager doesn't learn something about the employee, the operation, working conditions and so on, then it is probable that the session has not been a complete success.

5 *Counseling requires follow-up.* It is not a one-time event. If it is serious enough to require counseling, then it calls for a follow-up. Whatever the manager and subordinate agree to must be monitored. If the desired change occurs, then the manager should reinforce it. If it doesn't come about, then more discussion between manager and employee is called for.

6 *Counseling is an investment.* It is time and effort invested to improve the effectiveness of an employee, thereby raising the overall effectiveness of the work group. As in the case of appraisal, counseling is not grudge time. The focus is on the future: How can we raise the level of your performance? How can you and we get what we want from your efforts? The past, as we'll see, does need to be talked about. But the emphasis is on making the subordinate a more valuable, more productive, member of the group. Thus, every day that counseling is indicated and is delayed means less chance to enjoy dividends from your investment in that employee.

7 *Be prepared to refer elsewhere if necessary.* Most managers are ill prepared to do certain kinds of counseling. Problems involving emotional difficulties, drug or alcohol abuse, family conflicts, and the like are usually beyond the ability of the manager to handle. You may find yourself in the middle of such a problem while dealing quite legitimately with a performance deficiency. When you recognize that the employee's on-the-job behavior is influenced by such a personal factor, don't try to advise or play Dutch uncle. You have a right to insist that the subordinate seek help in order to improve work performance, but you can't provide that help. An employee who is wrestling with a severe personal problem may try to enlist your aid, either from desperation or in an attempt to win sympathy. Be prepared to refer the employee elsewhere for professional counsel.

The counseling sequence

Counseling is hardly an off-the-cuff activity. It calls for skill. There's a recommended sequence to be followed in dealing with an employee with performance problems:

1 *Your preparation.* You should have some objective evidence of the problem—insufficient sales calls made, unusually high turnover in a department, a falling off in work units produced, etc. In fact, considering today's antidiscrimination laws, you can't afford not to have documentation in case you have to terminate a subordinate for poor performance. Even aside from legal considerations, you need evidence that the subordinate can accept. Otherwise, you may spend the entire counseling session arguing with the employee about whether your interpretation of the performance data is valid.

The preparation, therefore, is a necessary step, especially since it has the virtue of discouraging an impromptu counseling session when the employee does something that irritates the manager. The need for focus cannot be overemphasized. Once again, I point out the danger of a laundry list: Just in case the subordinate doesn't accept one particular problem, some managers are careful to have a record of thirteen other problems in the hope that they can score with at least one. The experience can seem to the employee as a vendetta. The result is more often employee resentment than a correction of problem behavior.

In your preparation, concentrate on the critical issue to be resolved. You may find it difficult to keep both of you focused on that one behavior change without dragging in issues that can lead you far away. If you meet resistance, you may want to introduce additional evidence that the employee has a problem.

2 *State the problem.* "We agreed that you would produce $50,000 in new business by July. Here it is October and you are still $3,000 short of that objective. Don't you agree that we ought to talk about this?"

Now your preparation becomes very useful. The subordinate accepted a goal, a measurement, a project, and he or she hasn't brought it off. The two of you have a problem.

In stating the problem, stick to behavior or performance. Stay away from attitudes and other intangibles that can't be measured. Don't make judgments: "I thought we were working together, but apparently you're just not interested in cooperating." Such is the statement of a manager who is already exasperated and probably on the way to becoming even more so. Aside from being offensively judgmental, the tone is accusatory. Someone charged with a crime will rush to defense. You want to solve a problem, not run a courtroom. Ironically, if you accuse, you may wind up having to defend yourself.

To avoid an accusatory tone, you may wish to state your perception or understanding and check it out. "As I understand it, you were going to have the restructuring of the department all set up by November 1st and then we were going to . . . Was that your understanding?" There may be any number of things that have occurred, or obstacles that have arisen. Besides which, the subordinate, as you now discover, may not have had that understanding at all.

Whatever you do, don't proceed beyond this point without an agreement that you both have something to talk about. Otherwise, you may find yourself giving a speech or becoming locked in a futile debate. If the subordinate doesn't think the terms you have used describe the issue, then invite the employee to help you find more acceptable words: "Okay, maybe I've misunderstood. Tell me how you see the situation."

I am not by any means saying that the counseling session must stop if the subordinate doesn't agree on an obvious problem. For example, he has been coming in thirty minutes late two and three times a week when everyone else is expected to be on time—and, generally speaking, *is.* He may say, "I just don't regard being in here at the stroke of nine that important. It's what I do while I'm here that's essential." Now you have an issue: You have different priorities. You have that to agree on.

3 *Listen.* Accept the probability that the subordinate has a story to tell and then let him or her tell it without being interrupted by a rebuttal. And give sufficient opportunity for the subordinate to vent his or her emotional reaction to what you have said. Remember that a negative reaction is normal and usually precedes one that is positive. After stating the problem, you may have a fight on your hands; the subordinate may withdraw—be there physically but not rationally or emotionally—or may offer rationalization.

You don't have to agree with anything that goes on. If you sit it out, you're not necessarily endorsing the negative response. You are, however, indicating to the employee under stress that you understand how the person feels. If you can't accept this person and his or her feelings, your chances of building a solution acceptable to both of you are extremely slim.

4 *Consider the extenuating circumstances.* Keep in mind that the person's explanation of the problem may not be entirely rationalization. Consider the possibilities below, for starters:

Change in situation. Working conditions may have altered since the objectives or standards were set. The location of the work place, the people involved, the flow of the work, all may have contributed to the problem. You may have to corroborate the employee's version, but unless you are certain the excuse is flimsy, don't dismiss it without checking.

Insufficient knowledge or skill. Neither you nor the subordinate may have known at the outset what was really required to do the job. You may now decide that the choice of person was wrong or that training, help, or equipment can be provided to get the job done.

Workload. Look for a change in workload that may have resulted in a disproportionate accountability. The saleswoman who is asked to undertake a regional market research project, or to cover temporarily a portion of another territory, while maintaining her primary responsibility, may have a justification for a performance deficiency.

Conflict with co-workers in your department or in another with which your subordinates must cooperate. It's possible that your subordinate may be in part responsible for the conflict, but the conflict has become a factor that interferes with getting the work done. It has to be dealt with in the counseling process. You may not be able to eliminate the conflict entirely, but you may be able to help the subordinate to reduce his or her contribution to it.

Personal problems. Be ready to offer assistance in the way of referring the subordinate to the proper help. But while listening to an account of a personal problem, don't be diverted from your objective: to correct performance. You are on the employee's side, true, but the work still has to be done. Bear in mind, however, that counseling, as I've said, is a learning opportunity for you. Your records may not tell the whole story behind the performance problem.

5 *Look for the desired alternative.* Never forget that this is what the counseling is all about. The reason why the deficiency has occurred is probably important; but what you're going to do about it is even more so. "Okay, we both agree this is not the way we want it. What can we do about it? What would be a more effective way to do it?"

6 *Get agreement on the alternative.* "This is what we've agreed upon, right?" Describe it, then ask, "Do you see it that way?" Don't assume agreement *and* understanding. After all, you're the boss. A subordinate could be agreeing without understanding so as not to offend you.

7 *Design an action plan.* Now that you have agreed upon where you're headed, it is time to build the means to get there. "You're going to make three extra calls each week," or, "You're going to check with me whenever you have a problem with shipping, and we'll decide between us how we'll handle it."

The action plan concerns not only *what* is to be done but *how, when,* and by *whom*—if others are involved. Before concluding the session, be sure you design a plan that spells out measurement, schedule of review, and time of completion.

8 *Get the employee's perception* of what has happened and what will happen. For example, say, "Tell me how you see what we've agreed upon, just so you and I know that we are talking about the same thing." When the employee has summarized the discussion to your satisfaction, the session is over.

9 *Follow through.* I repeat: Counseling is not a one-time event. There are supposed to be results. If they are what you want, reinforce them. If they are not, consider whether another session may be necessary.

Counseling and you

One important aspect of counseling that needs to be dealt with is your own stress. The better documented and more confident you are in what needs to be done, the less stress you'll have in most cases.

Some managers cope with their feelings by voicing them. "This is causing me a great deal of discomfort." Or, "It upsets me to have to do this." "I don't know how you feel, but this is a very difficult thing for me." The greater your esteem and concern for the employee, the greater the stress you feel, and understandably so. You may not wish to verbalize it, but don't attempt to bury it. That just makes it work harder or in less obvious ways. It will do damage unless you at least acknowledge to yourself that you are tense.

If you are concerned that an employee might take advantage of your stress by trying to distract or sidetrack you, just make a note to yourself not to lose sight of your objective. Long sad stories, denials that the problem exists, etc. can't sidetrack you for long if you have proper documentation and are persistent.

Adding to your stress sometimes will be the feeling that as part of the employee's negative reaction, you are being counterattacked. After all, the employee may feel under attack. Lashing back at you may seem to be a good way to get you off the offensive. You'll need a lot of patience during this phase of the session—and many reminders that the employee is reacting in a fairly normal way.

Some managers try to reduce the stress by trying to control the employee's reaction. One way, of course, is to dictate to the employee what may or may not be said: "I don't think we should get into that," says the manager when the employee complains about problems she is having with a key person in the department. Another controlling device might be expressed as, "I'm not interested in the reasons"; yet another when a subordinate begins to show the real impact of the problem on him or her would be, "I think you should get a grip on yourself, and not allow yourself to become so emotional." This approach has disadvantages, though. If you try to control what the employee says, you may be preventing the person from giving you information you need. And you'll probably create resentment that will lead to further problems.

Managers who seek to control employees' reactions to counseling also try to filter out the more serious messages through diplomacy. For example: The true message is, "Your work is clearly unacceptable. It cannot continue this way"; what comes out is, "I know—and you do, too—that you're capable of far better work than you're doing, and I don't think I'd be fair to either of us not to try to help you improve." This manager is anxious not to offend. Unfortunately, the actual seriousness of the message gets lost in the verbiage.

Of course, managers sometimes try to exercise control because the employees begin to talk about personal problems that they believe influence on-the-job performance. Once again, the best response is for you to offer to refer the troubled employee to some professional help where the wife's drinking or the child's delinquency can be dealt with. You can also say, "I can't really help you with your problem, although I understand the strain under which you're working. I'm willing to give you every possible consideration—but at the same time, we have certain goals to meet. I'd like you to give some thought as to how you and I both can get what we need." You may be willing to rearrange the schedule or the assignments. You can be sympathetic without being "Dear Abby." And you can bring about solutions without becoming the family confidant, chiefly by being willing to find relief if the employee also takes some initiative.

In general, trying to control the employee's reaction will result in your hearing what you want to hear and not what you need to hear.

There are other ways in which managers inhibit their effectiveness in counseling. One is by rushing it, scheduling the session back-to-back with another appointment. You have to allow sufficient time for the proper counseling sequence.

True, there are better times for counseling than others. People differ on this, but my recommendation is early in the morning. That way the employee has time to work with you afterward, see that you are not hostile or biased against him or her. That normal working time is desirable, since it helps to demonstrate that you mean business when you say you are interested in helping the employee. It also helps to discourage any suspicion the subordinate may have that counseling is tantamount to punishing. By the time lunch arrives, some of the employee's tension and anger should have drained off— which should also discourage the subordinate from giving a hostile earful to co-workers.

Early in the afternoon is also acceptable if the employee doesn't have prior notice (and I don't believe the employee needs advance notice). You don't want an anguished subordinate getting sick over lunch, wondering what you're going to say or do. Late in the day is bad. The employee takes all the anxiety and anger home.

Besides rushing, there are other inhibitors—not being adequately prepared and not listening. Or not seeming to listen. So look at the employee, nod to show you are listening, and occasionally, if possible or desirable, refer to something the subordinate has said to show that you have indeed listened.

There's no way around it: Counseling is an anxiety-producer for the manager. It is a risk. It would seem much easier to assume that employees know when they do not perform well. It's easier to convince oneself that counseling might seem to employees like an invasion of privacy.

But counseling is an investment. Many employees

need it at one time or another. If they sense that they need it, and if you don't provide it, they can become demoralized and de-motivated. On your side, you cannot properly utilize and develop the resources of the people who report to you without incorporating counseling into your feedback program.

13: Criticizing for results

"**I** know when I make a mistake; I seldom hear when I do things right." Recite that familiar complaint to a room full of managers, and you'll get a room full of heads nodding in agreement. (Interestingly, I find, they're often expressing not only how they're treated by their bosses, but admitting their behavior toward their subordinates as well.)

Many managers—probably most—seem to be more conscientious about criticizing mistakes than acknowledging accomplishment. And, in a way, that's understandable. After all, when something is done wrong or poorly, it fairly cries out for action. It needs to be corrected. Something that is done right or well may make little noise.

Too, managers who are reluctant to praise good performance may have a bit of the military in them. If you were an enlisted person in the service, you may recall that, when an inspecting officer told you your equipment was especially clean, it was a mistake to reply, "Thank you, sir." The officer would very likely snap back, "Don't thank me. That wasn't a compliment. It's supposed to be clean!" Managers will adopt this line of thought: "Why should I compliment a subordinate for doing something the way it's supposed to be done?"

One answer, of course, is that people value being recognized, especially by someone whose esteem is important to them. It's a rare employee who doesn't respond favorably to a manager's expressing, "I appreciate the fine job you are doing." Employees who are deprived of positive reinforcement may actually seek negative feedback. Among training professionals there is the well-known story of the salesman who refused to send his sales call reports in on time. Every few weeks his manager would telephone and chew him out for being late with his reports. It was the only recognition his manager ever extended to him. Apparently, the periodic bawling out was better than neglectful silence.

Furthermore, when a manager gives a subordinate positive feedback on the employee's work, the manager is reaffirming standards. It's a way of saying, "This is the way I like to see the work done. Please keep it up." The manager gets an important message across and gives pleasure at the same time. I repeat: It is a mistake to assume that employees always know when they are performing well.

A reaffirmation of your standards can be very important to a subordinate's feeling of well-being on the job. It increases a person's confidence and sense of security to know that he or she is doing the work as it should be done (or at least as you want it done). When you acknowledge good performance, you reduce the floundering, the waste of energy, the demoralization that occurs when employees wonder what they should be doing—and how.

Giving positive feedback or praise to a worthy employee encourages other subordinates to perform well. They have the assurance that, when they do a good job, they'll be recognized for doing it. Incidentally, a manager's feedback may stimulate employees to give one another feedback. Peer recognition can be a potent reinforcer.

Mixing criticism with praise

Criticism can also be a form of recognition, as the salesman who was always late with call reports understood.

At the very least, the manager is saying to the employee, "I realize that you are here." In Transactional Analysis terms, criticism can constitute stroking, an acknowledgment that the other person exists, and that his or her existence has a value.

A manager who criticizes effectively can convey this additional message: "I know you want to do a good job. That's why I am criticizing you—to help you perform in a better manner." Unfortunately, much criticism does not give such a clear message.

Criticism is seldom without pain, and managers dilute it to try to reduce that pain. The *sandwich technique* of criticism is a good example of dilution. I define the sandwich as a slab of criticism between two slices of praise. Here's an illustration of a manager using it:

The manager calls Tim into his office to say, "I thought I was overdue in having a talk with you. You know, Tim, it's very easy to let a lot of time go by and give you the impression that I take you for granted. Your work has been so consistently of high quality, and you know what they say about squeaking wheels. I have a few of those, and that's why it is such a pleasure to have you around. You know, I'm not embarrassed to tell you how much I respect your conscientiousness, which is why I feel I would betray that respect if I didn't mention one small matter. I can't help noticing lately that some of your lunch hours have been a bit long. You probably aren't even aware of it. Heaven knows I don't mind in your case, Tim, but the problem is that some of the others in the department may get the idea that they can take off as much as they like. Again, I don't want to make a big deal of this, but I knew you'd understand. You've always been very discreet, very sensitive. One word is usually enough."

Tim can't be blamed if he walks out of that office a bit confused. At first he may feel pleasure over the nice words and only a little sting. Later he may begin to feel resentful as it dawns on him that the long lunch hours was not an incidental matter, as the boss tried to make it. It did not just come to mind in the middle of a nice, friendly discussion.

Why didn't the boss just come right out and say, "Tim, I'd like you cut down on some of those long lunch hours"? Probably because the boss told himself that he wanted to spare good old Tim any pain. He would encapsulate the criticism so thoroughly that it would be down before Tim could taste the bitterness. In truth, the boss wanted to save himself some pain as well. "I don't like to criticize Tim. He won't like it either. How can I make it easier for both of us?"

As you can see, the problem with the sandwich technique is that you dilute the criticism with praise and contaminate the praise with criticism. What may result is not the change of behavior that the manager wants but a case of resentment that the manager certainly does not want. The person who walks away from the manager is a disgruntled employee who suspects the boss has pulled a con job.

I am *not* saying that a manager should always avoid mixing praise with criticism, though generally speaking, I do think it is a good idea if it can be avoided. True, there are some people who cannot seem to take their criticism straight. It seems to devastate them. Others have psychological defenses so strong that at the first seemingly negative word their filters close and nothing gets through. It's probable that the only way a manager can successfully criticize such a person is carefully and obliquely. But that is unfortunate. And it is doubtful whether it is often successful. What is fortunate is that such people are rare, far more so than most managers realize.

There are occasions, however, when a manager must mix positive and negative feedback. That's usually when time is a factor. After all, a sales manager who sees a particular salesperson once every six months may see some problems in the person's way of doing things that need urgent attention. But the manager certainly doesn't want the rare visit to have a totally negative tone. Nor should the salesperson have to wait for the praise.

The question is, which should come first, the bad news or the good? Or should they be mixed up? There are those who advocate covering the positive aspects first so as to get the person who is about to be criticized in a good mood. In other words, to disarm the subordinate. But if the other person suspects that criticism is waiting in the wings, then the chance is slim that he or she will drop the barriers. And some important positive statements may not be heard; or if they are heard, they may not be accepted.

Keep the message clear

My recommendation is that the negative part come first in the feedback session. For example, Sheila has problems asking her sales prospect for the order. That is a serious deficiency. She senses it. Burt, her boss, points this out to her first thing without trying to protect her from pain. (The irony is that often the subordinate, as Sheila does, knows he or she needs criticism; the pain is already there. The manager's attention and criticism can often relieve that pain.)

After Burt and Sheila agree on what she has to do to correct her weakness in closing, the manager goes on to reinforce what she does well. "I notice that you very quickly establish rapport with prospects. They're ready to listen to you. Your presentation is very convincing. You come across as a very credible person. There's no reason why you can't become one of our best salespeople."

Burt does not return to the negative. It would be very easy to append the cautionary ". . . if you work on those closing techniques." If he made the point earlier, why should he allude to it again and detract from the positive statements?

When you have to mix negative and positive feedback, try to keep them separate: negative first, then positive. Don't return to the negative, if you can help it. You risk confusing the signals.

Be honest with the proportions. If the negative is a major issue, say so: "I'm about to comment on some aspects of the work you do very well, but before I leave the negative side, let's both understand that the problem I've described is very serious and has to be corrected." (It's when the problems dominate that the manager may feel the greatest temptation to reemphasize the negative after the positive. But if the manager does use the counseling techniques described in the previous chapter and nail down the action taken, there is little or no need to take away from the positive by returning to the negative.) Or it could go the other way. "Look, I want you to know that this is a minor deficiency. Work on it, but it's not a life-and-death issue. Now let's turn to the many things you're doing right."

Guidelines for criticizing

"You just don't seem to have the proper attitude toward your work." How many times have you heard such criticism about people's attitudes or characteristics? "She's a bit on the lazy side"; or, "He lacks loyalty." As I discussed in the chapter on performance appraisal, evaluating someone's attitudes, traits, characteristics, or motives is a highly subjective and risky business. If as a manager you try to characterize or attach labels, you may find yourself quickly and deeply mired.

Of all the rules of effective criticism, the first has to be this: *Stick to behavior.* Behavior can be seen. "You have a poor attitude toward work" may be arguable. But, "You have been more than fifteen minutes late to work three days this week" is not. "You ought to respect your co-workers" may not get you the response and results you look for. But when you point out to your disrespectful subordinate that he has a habit of interrupting people when they're talking in meetings, you've said something that can be easily verified.

When you criticize, therefore, talk about behavior or performance characteristics. Being absent, missing deadlines, turning out work that has to be redone, creating conflicts with other employees, these are things that can't be disputed. *Why* they happened is something else. You and the subordinate have to decide whether you want to get into causes. But you're on safer ground if you avoid labeling, characterizing, or defining motives.

Here are some other recommendations for building more impact into your criticism:

1 *Criticize as quickly as possible* after the mistake or the omission has occurred or the deficiency has become evident. You want the employee to learn from what has happened or is happening. You can be more precise in describing what you find objectionable, and the employee can be more clear in remembering what has happened if you seize the first opportunity to give feedback. There's also less chance that the offensive behavior will be repeated if you call attention to it immediately. If the employee realizes even without your feedback that something is wrong, early criticism will reduce tension and anxiety. If the person is uptight, and if you let time pass, the employee may falter in other aspects of his or her performance.

2 *Be specific* about what you want to criticize—and stay with it. It's easy during an uncomfortable session of criticism to stray from the issue that prompted it. The subordinate tries to ease the discomfort by sidetracking the manager, for example, and telling a sad tale. "Well, you see, I've been having a lot of car trouble, and this one mechanic I've been going to . . ." You want the employee to come in on time. He wants to tell you about his car troubles that have kept him from being on time.

Managers also sidetrack themselves. Instead of restricting the discussion to a specific fault, the manager will try to justify the criticism by bolstering it with other examples. "This isn't the only time. Three months ago, you . . ." or, "There are some other things you do that I find equally exasperating." First thing the manager knows, there's a whole laundry list on the table. Every event or bit of data introduced provided opportunities for argument or at least discussion. What the manager wanted to call attention to at the outset is buried, even forgotten. Managers have to learn to say at the threat of digression, "Yes, I understand, but this is the problem that I think we should stick with. Let's work on that."

3 *Get the employee's agreement* that a problem exists. There's nothing more ego-deflating for a manager than to let loose a lot of criticism only to have an employee shrug and say, "I don't see the problem," or, "I can't understand why you're so excited."

A sounder approach is to spell out what is bothering you and why. "I asked you three days ago about that report that was supposed to go to personnel. You told me you'd get it out no later than yesterday. Yet personnel didn't get it, and Natalie told me this morning that you'd given her only the first page to type. You are already two days late. I think we have a problem to discuss. Do you agree?" Presenting the issue this way precludes or at least lessens the room for argument.

4 *Look for alternatives.* Much time in criticism sessions is often spent looking for the *why* behind an offensive behavior. Employees will say to me, "My boss is much more interested in blaming me for what went wrong than he is in finding better ways." The boss may not, in fact, be more interested in blame than in improvement. But that's the message that employees receive.

Sometimes, searching for cause or motives can go to absurd lengths. In one Manhattan office, for example, the rule was that all desks had to be locked each day at the end of work. A guard later tested all desk drawers. If one was found unlocked, the employee assigned to it was left a printed form: "Your desk was found unlocked. Why did you forget to lock it?"

Motives for forgetting probably are best left to a therapist to uncover.

Once you get agreement that a problem exists, or that consequences call for action, get help in looking for solutions. Here's a criticism session between Joan and her subordinate, Chris.

> *Joan:* I just had a call from the production manager. He says one of his people asked us to expedite an order and that you refused. He also said that you were very rude.

> *Chris:* Henry called me about that order. That guy has no manners. He doesn't ask. He tells you what he wants. Well, I don't work for him. I've got orders piled three feet deep on my desk and I'm not going to stop everything and look for one order just because Henry wants it. I told him to shove it and hung up.

> *Joan:* You hung up? Do you think that's how we should treat people in other departments?

> *Chris:* No. It's not right. I know that. But if you had to put up with Henry's arrogance as much as I have to, you'd lose your cool, too.

> *Joan:* Okay. We have a problem. You and Henry don't get along too well. The production manager is upset. Is that a fair description?

> *Chris:* I guess so.

> *Joan:* Well, production needs us, and we have to get along with them. Now how do you think we can achieve that?

Note that Joan is more interested in how to get better interdepartmental cooperation than in assigning blame. As a general rule, assigning blame or searching for motives is not nearly so constructive as saying, "This is the problem. Neither of us likes the present situation. How could we make it better?"

Criticizing in public

"Praise in public; criticize in private." That's typical of the many managerial axioms that are taken for granted. Like the rest, it bears questioning. If you are tempted to criticize an erring subordinate before others, what is your motive? In some cases, you may not have time to analyze it. You are angry. One manager, in a meeting of her staff, learned that the filing of an important application had been delayed. Through questioning of various subordinates around the table, she identified the person whose carelessness resulted in their having missed the filing date. She lost her temper and bawled out the subordinate before his co-workers.

That happens. People understand it as an honest emotion, a natural reaction. But what about the chastised subordinate? The manager's only recourse was to apologize—publicly. Later in the meeting she said to the employee, "I lost my temper, and I embarrassed you before the group. I'm sorry for that. I think you and I ought to get together after the meeting to talk about how we can salvage the situation."

Her intention really hadn't been to punish the subordinate. But there are times when that seems to be the intention of the manager who exposes a sin in public. The exposure may indeed discourage a repetition. It may also serve to announce that people who make mistakes will be confined to the stocks in the square. Thus, people will try to avoid mistakes, which may result in their doing as little as possible.

Most public criticism will be seen as punitive. Can it ever be constructive? In a few specific circumstances— when there is a problem to which everyone needs to be alerted—safety, for example. One employee has regularly misplaced his safety glasses, something that others do periodically. You may wish to make an example of him by criticizing him in front of others who are also tempted occasionally to be careless.

Another use of public criticism that could bear fruit is taking the consistently poor performer to task. One of the secretaries, for example, disappears into the women's room several times a day for long stretches of time. You've warned her privately, but your warnings have been disregarded. The fact that she flouts you is widely known. You wait near her desk, and when she reappears, you say, "I've wasted much valuable time trying to speak with you, and you haven't been at your desk for the last twenty minutes. From now on, I have to insist that you not be absent from your work station for more than ten minutes at a time without permission."

Your message, delivered publicly, will have a double effect: One, you'll tell her that you mean business; two, you'll let everyone else know that also. And the latter is important, because they have probably resented the fact that you have apparently let her get away with her long disappearances.

In general, however, unless you believe that public criticism will have a constructive effect, either on the erring subordinate or on others, avoid it.

A learning opportunity

Criticism is obviously a learning experience for the person receiving the feedback. But it should be so for the criticizer as well. If you do not see criticism as a learning opportunity for you, you could be missing much. For one thing, you may lose out on the opportunity to uncover some organizational problems you didn't know existed. It's true that you don't want to get sidetracked in a criticism session. But it is equally true that you don't want to ignore related problems that cry out for attention. Your discussion with the employee who needs some negative feedback may uncover a variety of problems. "I can't get the report you wanted me to do because the only person who can give me the data I need on media has been holed up in his office practically drunk every day." Or, "It would help if I could talk to Jim directly, but his boss insists I deal with Jim through him. And everything takes three days longer to do."

You might even discover that you are part of the problem—if you are fortunate. For example, an employee may say, "Yes, I agree, the job wasn't done right. But I needed help, and every time I came to you, you just patted me on the shoulder and told me you were sure I'd do a good job. I needed information, and you gave me encouragement."

As with counseling, criticism is an investment. If the work is to be done as you want and need it to be done, you have to insist that behavior that gets in the way be corrected. The sooner, the better.

Criticism is considerate. The employee wants to do the work as it should be done. Your feedback, even though it is negative, is necessary and welcome because it guides the employee to better results.

14: Reinforcing the results

When subordinates are not doing a good job, you criticize them to help them find ways to improve their performance. But how do you let subordinates know when they're doing well—or better than before? You reinforce them positively.

In encouraging effective performance, there is no more potent tool available to you than *positive reinforcement*. It is an important part of your feedback program. But positive reinforcement offers a double payoff. It is a reward for past performance.

In chapter 7, I have already described many kinds of rewards and reinforcers there are at your disposal. (You've probably come up with a few that you hadn't previously identified as such.) If you can use them regularly to recognize the performance you want from subordinates, you are more likely to encourage repetition of that performance than if you don't reinforce. Thus, positive reinforcement helps you to recognize and reward past performance and perpetuate it.

Positive reinforcement is a phrase that gets a lot of kicking around these days. Some people refer to its origin as rat or pigeon psychology. True, it is a child of the laboratory, identified with the famous American psychologist, B.F. Skinner. He taught pigeons to pick at levers to obtain food, which was the reinforcement.

The scientific name for a positive reinforcement program is operant conditioning. Skinner concluded that people can also be conditioned to perform certain functions or behaviors if those behaviors are reinforced or rewarded. Unfortunately, in the minds of many people (including some psychologists) the word condition has become synonymous with control.

Recently another term, also related to operant conditioning, has become widely used, and not always favorably: behavior modification. Sometimes the phrase appears to be used interchangeably with brainwashing. It's true that both may result in behavior change. But there the relationship ends. Brainwashing creates victims. People do not normally submit to it voluntarily.

Behavior modification creates partners. The person sees a reason for changing. That reason, of course, must be real and have value. That is only one reason why management by manipulation—whereby managers try to obtain kinds of behavior by deception and by holding out suggestions of rewards they can't or don't intend to deliver—does not work. Most people are well attuned to the old saying, "You fool me once, shame on you; you fool me twice, shame on me."

In my view, positive reinforcement is a legitimate, effective, and necessary tool for the manager. It is used to reward desired behavior, to encourage its repetition and persistence. It can bring about a modification of behavior, from that which is ineffective to that which is effective. But it is only effective over the long term when the manager uses it conscientiously, honestly, openly, for the subordinate's well-being as well as for the organization's.

The use of praise

The positive reinforcer that is most available to you is praise. If you are like most managers, you do not take advantage of it as often as you could. Praise is the most available reinforcer—and probably the least used. It is a simple technique, though only simple if you know how. It costs no money. Those managers who use it well can testify to its effectiveness. When it is done right, praise has a ripple effect. Not only does it provide a reward—recognition for the person who is performing well—it broadcasts to the entire work group that good performance will be rewarded.

If praise as a positive reinforcer has all of these benefits, why don't managers use it more often? This is speculation, but I suspect that many otherwise experienced managers are skeptical: They don't really believe it works; and it may not—for them. Why?

For one thing, because those managers are not consistent in using it. In management, consistency can be a virtue. People really do prefer a degree of predictability in their bosses. When people perform well, expecting to be praised for it, and that praise is not forthcoming, people lose a little faith in their manager. A dangerous question may enter their minds: Does my boss really appreciate the effort? It's a very small step from that question to the relaxation of standards.

Thus, if praise is used correctly, it builds trust between manager and subordinate. If inconsistently applied as a reinforcer, it confuses and de-motivates. Thus, the manager who tries to reinforce through praise and does it poorly looks at the results and says, "You see, praise doesn't work well."

But there are other reasons why a manager may hesitate to accept what many are saying about the effectiveness of praise:

1 *It may appear manipulative.* True, it will appear to be manipulation if it isn't part of an understanding between manager and subordinate. That understanding is based upon a mutual realization that each is going to benefit from the subordinate's good performance. There is nothing wrong with the manager defining, helping, encouraging, guiding, and praising the performance of an employee. If everyone knows what is going on, there is no manipulation involved.

2 *Praise makes a manager vulnerable.* It does tend to reinforce a manager's dependency. But then, that would seem to be a given: Managers need subordinates. If subordinates realize it, and they do, the manager's recognition of it would seem to underline and honor the bond between them. There is a contract between boss and subordinate. It exists. Both know it exists.

3 *Praise may be construed as a promise.* This could be a real danger. Praise may be seen as a promissory note. For example, a manager says to a subordinate in a moment of genuine enthusiasm, "You know, there is a new division being formed in Illinois. If you keep up this kind of effort, I'm sure there'll be an important role for you to play in that division." That sort of reinforcement, especially if repeated, could build expectations in the employee's mind far above what the manager intends. If the "important role" that develops is not what the employee has come to expect, there could be trouble.

4 *Managers get too busy to praise.* This is probably the single most frequent problem of managers. They forget to say "thank you" for the performances they expect. Of course, when they don't get what they expect, they seldom forget to say something. Once a manager becomes proficient in positive reinforcement through praise, he or she will understand how much easier it is to influence the right kind of behavior while the work is being done than to have to criticize and correct after mistakes and deficiencies have become evident.

When praise misfires

As is true with any technique, praise, if applied carelessly or with insufficient thought, can create problems. Frequently the problem is that the praise is disproportionate. Or it is seen as disproportionate. One employee,

Paul, was transferred into Win's department. Paul could be characterized as one of life's losers. Win agreed to take him on for a last chance. To everyone's surprise, including Win's, Paul began to shed his loser image. Win reinforced every stage of Paul's progress. Seemingly, the more Win praised Paul, the more effective Paul became.

Win was overjoyed. Obviously he felt triumph. He had been able to accomplish with Paul what no other manager had. However, Paul could still be ineffective. His immediate supervisor assigned him an important data-gathering job. Paul turned it in on a Friday afternoon at four o'clock, then left for the weekend. The supervisor found to her dismay that Paul had not followed instructions. The consequence was that the supervisor was in the office until nine o'clock that evening correcting Paul's work. On Monday she complained to Win, who told her to let Paul know of his unsatisfactory work. But Paul refused to accept the criticism. He steadfastly argued that the supervisor had no right to criticize his performance. His self-esteem had been so strenuously reinforced that he could not accept the negative feedback.

In Paul's case that inability was unfortunate. But, as Paul's co-workers had realized already, Win's praise of Paul had been disproportionate. They resented it. They had recognized that Win's positive reinforcement of Paul had been in part self-congratulatory, which made Win lose some of his credibility with other subordinates.

You may have a tendency to praise highly if, as in the case of Paul, the person is an unusually difficult case who has never performed before as he or she is performing at the present. You may be tempted to overpraise a person of low self-esteem or self-confidence. Naturally, you want this occasion to stick out in his memory. So you pile it on. Then there are occasions when you just feel awfully good. You are up. You give a bonus of extra praise.

But what are the dangers? Credibility—first of all with the person being praised, resentment from the others.

The manager who is excessive too often, who praises loudly on routine accomplishments, has nowhere to go when exceptional performance occurs.

How to praise

Many of the guidelines for praising effectively—and rewarding in general—have already been mentioned. For example, *be consistent.* When praiseworthy performance occurs, don't miss the chance to recognize it. Soon people will understand that you recognize and reward good work. *Be honest.* Praise what is deserved. And be careful about suggesting rewards that you may not be able to deliver. *Be proportionate.* Praise doesn't cost anything, but it shouldn't be carelessly expended. Don't let irrelevant factors such as compassion determine how effusive your recognition is.

Other recommendations for praising effectively are:

1 *Be specific.* "You're doing a great job," or, "Keep up the good work," is probably better than no recognition at all. The problem is that it doesn't define what aspects of an employee's performance you like. For example, it is more helpful to tell a salesperson, "Charlie, I like your toughness. You really hang in there. Three times the prospect tried to get you out of the office, and each time you came back with another close."

To the subordinate who has written a clear, concise report, you may say, "You don't know how much I appreciate the way you made your point clearly and quickly. I didn't have to read several pages and wonder what it was all about."

The more specific you are about what you want and like, the greater the likelihood that it will be repeated.

Too, specificity prevents sameness or repetitiveness. The same general wording time after time gets tiresome and loses impact.

2 *Emphasize behavior.* Going back to the example of Charlie the salesman, the manager could have simply said, "I like your toughness." But that might not have given Charlie a clear indication of what aspect of his toughness was admirable. After all, toughness can be manifested any number of ways, desirable and undesirable.

It may be appropriate to praise someone's personality or traits: "You're popular with your co-workers." But that doesn't encourage repetition of important behavior. Instead, try, "The people who work with you tell me that you try to accommodate their requests whenever you can. And when you can't, you always give a full explanation. They tell me they like that." The subordinate knows what to continue to do.

3 *Praise soon after the event.* What is true in negative feedback is especially true in positive reinforcement. What the employee has done that is praiseworthy is fresh in his or her mind soon after. Recognizing the performance immediately offers greater insurance that the behavior will be repeated in the form you wish. Also, immediacy underlines your value of the specific performance. "Susan, I couldn't help overhearing you on the phone with that customer. Apparently he was furious. I like the way you calmly kept coming back to his practice of paying late and how that has caused his problems. Very good way to handle that kind of person."

Delayed recognition of performance sometimes conveys a by-the-way quality. It loses impact. There is the suggestion that the behavior wasn't really worth taking a moment to mention at the time.

Public vs. private praise

How public should you be with your praise? After all,
you want others in your work group to know that you
will recognize good performance. At the same time, you
don't want anyone to feel discriminated against. For
example, one manager put out a memo citing several
employees for meeting standards consistently. They
were pleased, but one employee was outraged. She reminded the manager that she had been disadvantaged
by having to work under certain constraints that the
others had not had to work under. There was some merit
to her case, although the manager felt she was rational-
izing a bit. Perhaps. But her feelings and perceptions
were important. She was de-motivated. The manager
admitted that he should have anticipated her reaction.
That is good advice: Try to anticipate how not only the
recipients of public praise, but also those who are not so
recognized, will respond.

Really outstanding performance by an individual
can usually be recognized publicly, especially if the performance has been exceptional for a long time. "Mary
Beth has led the unit in sales each year for five years in
a row." That is certainly not an accident. Mary Beth is
consistently doing something right—and that should be
noted.

When to go public with praise is not an easy matter
to define. For you, the manager, there are advantages
in public recognition of subordinates that will in turn
reflect favorably on you. But always ask yourself these
questions:

*Is the performance you praise something that
most others in the department can also achieve?* If it
is due largely to a particular talent not shared by others,
you are probably best advised to keep your praise private, directed solely to the talented performer.

*Have others in the work group been working
under constraints or restrictions that have reduced*

*their chances of duplicating the exceptional perform-
ance you are praising?* They may feel disadvantaged
when you praise someone who is free of the restraints
they have experienced. Consider then the possible de-
motivating effects of your public praise.

The necessity of trust

I am sometimes asked to define the difference between
stroking, as the term is used by Transactional Analysis,
and positive reinforcement. All positive reinforcement is
stroking, but not all stroking is positive reinforcement
of behavior. Essentially stroking is a recognition of another person. A warm hello or "It's nice to see you" are
examples of stroking, but they are not positive reinforcement.

For both stroking and reinforcement to be accepted,
which is to say, to be effective, there must be a trusting
relationship between manager and subordinate. For the
subordinate to respond favorably to positive reinforcement, he or she must feel the manager is sincere in the
praise.

Esteem is also an important factor. The subordinate
must hold the manager in reasonably high esteem, otherwise the praise may have little impact. This has little
to do with whether an employee *likes* the boss. But the
respect and esteem must be there.

Finally, an observation for the manager: Effective
positive reinforcement through praise of subordinates
will reinforce not only their behavior but yours. When
your praise leads to better performance by subordinates, the results will constitute a reward for your
efforts. Your use of positive reinforcement will grow.

15: Rewarding the right behavior

Reward the behavior you want; don't reward the behavior you don't want.

Does that statement seem obvious? It is. But it is also one of the most important management principles in this book. In fact, if you were to take nothing more from this book than that statement, and if you were to apply it regularly and conscientiously, you would derive tremendous benefits. It is the essence of management to reinforce the behavior that is productive, that gets results; it is equally essential to avoid rewarding behavior that is unproductive, or that is not directly related to getting the results you want.

The principle is so simple, so obvious. And it is so frequently violated. Look around. You'll probably see people being rewarded for many things other than good performance. In fact, you may even see cases in which the wrong kind of behavior is being rewarded. Often there is a wide gap between what managers would like to do, indeed, think they are doing—and what they actually are accomplishing.

For example, employees often come to feel that they are rewarded for not doing anything exceptional. They may even be encouraged to perform in a mediocre manner. A rather extreme example of this was provided a few years ago by a highly technical company in the South that, hurt by a recession, laid off a large number of employees. But one of the managers who survived pointed out that the greatest casualties were among the worst *and* best performers. "I expected the misfits to go, not some of our most talented people." This is by no means unusual. The explanation is that a recession offers a company a chance to get rid of people they should have fired before. But what about the top people? They have become expensive. Because of their outstanding contributions to the organization, their pay becomes substantial. When the company needs to cut down on expenses, they cut the high earners out.

There's another reason. As one veteran of several purges said to me, "Many of these people at or near the top are more entrepreneurial than good organization people. They're used to being somewhat independent. In a crunch, you need people who will tighten up and take orders."

In such an organization, it's not difficult to read the message most employees get: If you want to hang on to your job, don't be too good or too bad in what you do. The result, most likely, is mediocrity.

But management doesn't have to fire people in order to achieve mediocre performers. There are other ways to achieve them through poorly awarded reinforcements. For example:

1 *Rocking the boat.* In some organizations, people who suggest changes that they believe would be beneficial receive the label of troublemaker. Their ideas threaten the way things have traditionally been done, or they infringe upon someone's power. Many times the troublemakers are not punished or terminated; they are isolated so that they can't have an impact. They are tolerated, not encouraged. They may be transferred or given jobs of lesser importance. Management stops listening to them. If they stick around long enough, they learn how futile it is to protest or to try to innovate. Other employees view the humiliation or the neutralization of the would-be innovator and conclude that it doesn't pay to rock the boat.

2 *Guilt.* Old Joe was passed over in the race for vice-presidency. Judging by his performance, he deserved to lose, even though he had been around for twenty years. But top management felt guilty about refusing to give Joe the position and prestige he had been hoping for. So they made up a fancy title, gave him a big raise and an attractive office with a private secretary. It might seem harmless, but what others in the company were taught was this: If you do a fair job and stick it out around here, you'll still get a nice piece of the cake. Joe's performance was nothing to brag about, and yet he could easily become the model for many.

Guilt rewards can become bizarre. Take the case of one manager who, though incompetent, was retained by his company for more than fifteen years in a responsible position. He had almost no leadership ability, and that deficiency was recognized by nearly everyone. Ironically, he was considered so incompetent that people actually felt sorry for him. He had a pleasant personality and performed small chores for his boss. Strangely enough, each year he requested substantial raises and usually received them.

Eventually, the management above the incompetent department head was changed. Still he survived because, by that time, his bosses were feeling guilty about having let him stay on for so long. No one had ever told him he wasn't a capable manager. Finally, when he reached the age of fifty-four, he was forced out. But, since he could take early retirement the following year, the company arranged for him to stay on the payroll. He stayed home, drawing full salary and benefits for those twelve months, until the pension could take over.

3 *Loyalty.* "Carl has been a faithful employee for twenty years. The only time he ever missed work was when his wife died, and the day after the funeral he was back at his desk." Faithful performance, as well as consistent attendance, may merit recognition. But any other person in Carl's department could turn out what he does in half the time. What Carl's loyalty is contributing to the organization may be a mystery to some of those other employees who see Carl rewarded so handsomely.

4 *Potential.* Recognition is frequently given not for what people do but for what the manager thinks they are capable of doing someday. "I know that Ellen isn't performing according to our expectations, but I feel she has the ability and I want to show her how much confidence I have in her." But, of course, if Ellen doesn't perform according to expectations, others will wonder why she gets all of those rewards.

5 *Friendship* is often reinforced by money or other kinds of rewards. It doesn't have to be a close relationship. The boss feels temperamentally or intellectually closer to some subordinates than to others. That's quite legitimate. But why should it be rewarded? In one department, the manager has lunch frequently with three employees with whom he obviously has close rapport. He seldom socializes with any other subordinate. Some of the best assignments in the department have been distributed among the three employees. Favoritism is the word other subordinates use. The three are not incompetent, but, in the eyes of co-workers, they are no more competent than others.

6 *Politics* is a less frequent reward, but it is discernible here and there. Fred has a friend in a high place in the organization—perhaps a relative. Fred's manager hopes to build a reservoir of good will with that highly placed person by bestowing rewards on Fred. Performance has little or nothing to do with it.

7 *Sex* also plays a role occasionally in the granting of rewards. When this occurs, it is usually blatant enough to require no explanation here.

Many rewards that are given for nonperformance considerations are rooted in good will and good intentions. They seem, for the most part, quite innocent. Cer-

tainly, even in the case of guilt or compassion or friendship, the act of giving nonperformance rewards is very
human. But accept the consequences of the reinforcement you are extending. Perhaps the greatest risk you
take is creating misunderstanding, both in the person
reinforced, who may place greater emphasis on behavior that is not necessarily related to productivity, and in
others on the work force who may begin to think that
how they perform is secondary.

It isn't my intention to say that you should never
recognize fine qualities and nonperformance traits in
valued employees. I do suggest that you recognize ex-
actly what you intend to reward. And that you let others
know. Be sure you know the answers to the following
questions:

*Does the employee understand what I am recog-
nizing with this reward? What will be the long-term
impact on him or her?* (For example, will the employee
feel encouraged to continue certain behavior that you
don't find necessarily helpful?)

*Do other employees understand what I am recog-
nizing? What will be the short-term as well as the
long-term impact on them?* (For example, will the
other employees feel resentful of my recognition of another?)

This is certain: In granting rewards for any reason,
you need to make sure that employees never lose sight
of the essential relationship between good performance
and rewards. They must know that, even if you recognize factors other than work results, you won't fail to
reward the latter.

Encouraging the behavior you want

When a salesperson is prospecting poorly, when a manager is abrasive toward co-workers, when a secretary
constantly misfiles important documents, your objective
is to help them to develop more effective ways of doing

things. But that isn't all. You want the more effective
behavior, once established, to be continued. In other
words, you want to shape new behavior, then maintain
it. You don't actually mold the behavior, of course, but
you play an important part in getting the job done.
When and how you give rewards are the keys.

The whole process of behavior modification should
be quite open. After all, you and the employee, in general, want the same thing. You want the employee to be
effective; so does the employee. No one wants to bumble
about, to be frustrated, to fail to get the proper results
from the effort invested. The fact that both of you want
the employee to grow in effectiveness forms the basis
for the contract between you.

It may be up to you to define the specific behavior
you want. "Frank, I want you to develop a prospect card
file of at least six hundred names, categorized by potential volume, geographical location, product line needed,
etc." Periodically you look over Frank's prospect file,
and as you note the extent to which he is following your
counsel, you remark on it. "Your prospect file is coming
along very well, Frank. I'm very impressed by the
thoroughness with which you have researched your
prospects."

During the shaping process, you want to reinforce
every major new development. "Your file seems to be
working, Frank. I've noticed that, because you've done
such a fine job of organizing by geographical location,
you spend less time traveling. For the last three weeks
you've upped your weekly average by three calls." That
is very specific reinforcement.

However, after the new behavior is well established,
has been shaped, it's time for a different kind of reinforcement. Now the need is to maintain the behavior.
Reinforcing the behavior each time it occurs would soon
lose impact. For example, the secretary who has been
encouraged to eliminate errors from the letters she
types would hardly appreciate hearing, "Wow, another

perfect letter," each time she brings one into her boss's office for a signature. Continuing consistent specific reinforcement would become offensive.

To maintain behavior, occasional reinforcement by you is recommended. For example, at the end of a quarter, Frank's manager writes him a letter. "I'm enclosing your quarterly bonus, which averages nearly 15 percent more money than your previous bonus checks. Much of this increase, I'm certain, is due to your new prospecting system. Of course, it gives me a lot of pleasure to see you make more money. But I know you must get great satisfaction from such a substantial achievement."

Frank's boss has rather neatly enhanced Frank's internal reward and provided two external reinforcers.

Most managers are probably much more efficient at shaping than they are at maintaining. They get busy and distracted. They forget. Finally they become aware, for example, that many of the warehouse people who had been encouraged to lift boxes in a certain way to avoid back injury are slipping into old habits. Worker's compensation claims are once again on the rise.

Variety is the key

Varying the timing of reinforcements is only part of the answer. Find a way to put more variety into the rewards you give. Perhaps now is a good time to review chapter 7. The lists of rewards can spark your thinking. It might be an appropriate occasion to offer that secretary, who has now been presenting you with perfectly typed letters, a brand new typewriter. Or a new chair. Perhaps new equipment isn't necessary, but it would be a potent reinforcer to say, "Carolyn, just in case you don't think I appreciate the fact that you continue to turn out the best-looking letters around, I want you to look at this catalog and tell me what kind of chair you'd like to have."

A final caution about the cumulative effect of the

rewards you give: Keep the accumulation proportionate to the value of the employee's work. If the dividends are excessive considering the investment, the employee may feel tension. For example, the subordinate might say to himself or herself, "I know I'm not really productive enough to justify all of this. I know it. When will they know it?"

Altruism, gratitude, and enthusiasm may lure the manager into the trap of giving excessive rewards.

Putting more system into your rewards

Make a list of your subordinates. After each name list the person's performance characteristics that contribute to getting the work done for the accomplishment of your objectives. How recently have you recognized that performance? How regularly have you rewarded the behavior you want?

Next, review the kinds of rewards that are described in chapter 7. Of how many of these have you availed yourself?

What you will probably find is that you are not *regularly* and *predictably* recognizing the good work that people do.

Furthermore, don't be surprised if you discover that you have been reinforcing with only a fraction of the rewards available to you.

Keep in mind that increasing the value of the work requires continuing effort. But the payoff in productivity is well worth it.

16: Training, the key to effectiveness

One traditional definition of the manager's job is to get things done through people. If you examine that statement closely, you'll find it inadequate. A manipulative manager can get things done through people for a time. But that kind of manager neglects the obligation to build resources for the future. (In fact he or she destroys them.) No organization can be static and function well. Resources that are adequate today will probably be inadequate tomorrow. If they become so, clearly the manager has not done a good job.

Change, which characterizes our society and economy, demands growth in people to meet its challenges. (Whether the changes in our systems over the past thirty to forty years have all been for the better is open to question. What is certain is that they have led to greater and greater complexity.)

What about the old managerial axiom that people resist change? I don't accept it. People do resist what they suspect is being done *to* them. When a change is pending, it's a good move to explain what it is and how it will affect subordinates. Unfortunately, some managers play games or public relations at this point. They try to minimize the impact of unfavorable change—for example, a cutback in budget or people, relocation or transfer, a change in responsibilities—either by withholding information or by camouflaging the truth with a flow of words. Neither tactic works for long. And the damage to the manager's credibility may endure long after the change. It's a self-fulfilling prophecy: The manager decides that people will resist the change, so he or she tries to disguise it. People see through the screen and react resentfully. The manager has proved once again that people don't like change.

People will accept change if they are brought to see the benefits of that change to them. They will accept even an unpleasant change if it seems the least unfavorable of the options. At first they may decline to accept it. But they will come around when the truth is presented straightforwardly, if only because people accept change as a necessary factor in growth. Without change there would be no growth.

Growth is natural to people.

Frederick Herzberg maintains that growth is seen by employees as *good*. In his view, growth is a motivator. Abraham Maslow refers to self-actualization— becoming what one is capable of being, transforming potentiality into actuality—as a growth need. Most people feel the need to be stretched. If they feel that the work has any purpose or meaning at all, they would prefer to do it well rather than poorly. Most people, it's safe to say, would like to feel that what they do well today, they can do better next month. And that perhaps by next month, they will be learning to do some tasks and functions they cannot perform now. Thus, most people want to be effective on the job now—and to grow in effectiveness.

That's the manager's job: to increase the effectiveness of subordinates, to continue to help them to sharpen their ability to carry out the manager's objectives.

The real implications of this were brought home to me vividly a few years back when the training director of a well-known insurance company said to me: "Supervision is a function of training." That really perplexed me. At first I thought that he had come up with a catchy slogan, the kind that attracts attention but doesn't bear thinking through.

It also occurred to me that he was compensating for a feeling of powerlessness in his staff role. That is, training should be regarded by everyone as the most important function of the organization because he would like it so.

But what he said was neither a slogan nor a compensation. I think he made a valuable point, even though I suspect that most people would agree with the reaction of a man who for a number of years was one of the best-known names in supervisory and managerial training. When I repeated the training director's assertion, his eyebrows lifted. "I think he has it backwards," he responded. "Training is a function of supervision—one of them."

That is, unfortunately, the traditional—and still prevailing—view of training, development, and education. There's not much question about the place of training and development in most organizations—it is one function among many and not always considered a very important one at that. Training and development departments swell and shrink, come and go, depending upon the economy, the money available, the degree of management's with-itness, or the sales ability of training personnel.

Sometimes a training function is mostly a maintenance operation—making sure that the organization's traditions, procedures, and values are perpetuated. One occasionally encounters the grudging recognition that you really have to have some kind of training, development, and education program to keep your best people from going elsewhere. Too many organizations, in my view, seem content just to have a training program; but there is relatively little examination of what it is, what it is supposed to do, and whether it is really doing it.

The organization as a learning laboratory

Actually the entire organization is a learning laboratory that cannot successfully achieve its objectives until every member is learning effectively—and until every manager plays a key role in his or her employees' growth and progress on the job.

The most effective learning takes place in the working environment. Thus, the implications for training and development and management education are staggering; the challenge to traditional views of development and education in organizations is wrenching.

Each member of an organization is engaged every day—or should be—in some phase of improvement of effectiveness. And each manager is responsible for making sure—as only the manager can—that those who report to him or her take advantage of all growth and learning opportunities. The manager's function, then, is to see that employees are increasingly effective in achieving organizational goals.

Further, employees can be effective only if they can deal with almost constantly changing conditions, which usually means proceeding from a point that is known to one that is less known. The effective operation is one in which employees are able to analyze and diagnose each new variable and develop ways of dealing with it. All members of the organization, therefore, are in an unceasing learning situation, whether they realize it or not. How effective the employee is depends upon how well he or she learns to sharpen or alter a skill to meet the new demand.

At the center of all this is the manager, coaching, appraising, counseling, supervising the learning and growth. Or to put it another way, providing and reinforcing learning through managerial functions such as control, delegation, assignments, and problem solving.

Training is too important to be left solely to trainers. Trainers, educators, and consultants should be seen as resources. But the manager is the key to employees' growth. The trainer or consultant works with the manager to determine the growth needs of employees and to decide on the steps to be taken to meet those needs. But it is the manager, above all, who must accept the responsibility for upgrading the skills and knowledge of subordinates, for providing them with a sense of progress on the job. The manager's knowledge of employees guides him or her to establish their learning needs— technical or administrative skills, conflict resolution techniques, training in supervising a work group, problem-solving or decision-making methods. The manager works with the trainer to come up with an education program that will help employees to learn how to perform these new skills or apply the new knowledge *on the job*.

Most people probably would agree that they—and their organizations—still are a long way from such a learning system. Or are even a long way from recognizing that their organizations can function in this way. But the widespread practice of burdening the trainer with the chief responsibility for meeting the learning needs of members of the organization tends, at the least, to waste training dollars, and at the worst, to perpetuate the obstacles to organizational effectiveness.

Why trainers can't always train

If it is true that much of what is called training does not contribute to effectiveness, then everyone in a position of responsibility within an organization may have to bear some of the burden. The trainer can't be blamed— solely. In most organizations the trainer's job is to see that certain content is provided. Whether that content is relevant or applicable, whether it can in fact help the employee to increase his or her effectiveness, is usually beyond the educator's province.

Much of the fault lies in our perception of learning.

Education in this country, in and out of industry, in the lives of most people, is fragmented, compartmentalized, deductive. Traditionally, education is provided in stages, in definite locales—such as classrooms—by people designated as educators. In the minds of most people, certain dichotomies persist—theory and practice, classroom and the "real world." A government trainer explained to me, "The employee gets the theory in the classroom, and then we think he ought to have time to put the theory into practice back on the job."

I asked, "What steps do you take to find out whether he is applying the 'theory,' and how do you let him know how well he has applied it?"

After a moment of silence, the answer was, "No steps."

Actually what goes on in the classroom may have little or no relevance to the situation or the environment in which the learner works. The trainer may be confined to a classroom, going through motions of dubious value with a program or course that reflects the educator's values or perceptions of reality, which often are what *should* be rather than what is. The instructor's training design may be one that he or she has been able to get management to approve, that is, one that is safe, does not threaten the organization's traditions or policies. Or it may be one that the trainer has brought or borrowed from a different organization that has a different culture.

Often trainers are well aware that their assessment of the needs of the organization is in conflict with the way that management sees them. Then you hear sentiments similar to the ones I heard from a frustrated trainer: "I don't like the program I'm running. I designed it, they seem to like it, but I don't think it does much for anyone."

On the other hand, trainers often come to the training situation prepared to impart their values, what they perceive to be the needs of the learner, or what the organization's management wishes them to impart, which may not in the least meet the learner's needs.

The employees who are to be trained come to the learning situation with their own values. They want the content of the session to be consistent with behaviors that are comfortable to them and that they believe are rewarded by the organization.

Too, the learner most frequently comes to a training situation with disappointingly low expectations that are born of past experience with relatively unproductive sessions. Employees often suspect that they will encounter little resemblance between the training and work environments. As they often find that no effort is made to overcome the effects of conditioning or values they have acquired in the past, they themselves do not unfreeze their old behavior patterns. Once back in the work environment, they resume the patterns because they believe those behaviors will bring them rewards. And they are probably correct. After all, what the trainer has thought important may not be thought so by the learner's managers.

How people learn

For those reasons, the manager is pivotal to the learning of subordinates. Everything that research in adult learning has come up with points to this. And what the researchers have discovered relates very closely to what has already been said in this book about motivation in general.

There are five basic criteria for increasing effectiveness on the job:

1 *A reason for learning.* It's not enough to say, "I want you to take a course in instructional methods." You may have a reason, but it may not carry much value with the subordinate. Another approach might be, "I've noticed that when newer employees ask you for help,

you seem to have a talent for showing them how we do things here. How would you feel about taking this workshop on instructional methods and then setting up an orientation class—which you'd conduct—for new employees?" That is a value that the employees may more readily accept.

2 *The assurance of learning.* You might have to convince the employee that he or she has the ability to learn the new skill. For example, how many times has the subordinate displayed the talent, however undeveloped? "You seem to have a knack for this kind of work. That's why I'm selecting you for this training session. Since you show a natural ability, you'll have a leg up on the subject." You may also want to reassure the subordinate by describing how many other employees of varied abilities finished the training successfully.

3 *A chance to apply.* Employees in learning situations need opportunities to practice. The practice completes and reinforces the learning. One of the biggest drawbacks to learning away from the work situation is that there is a time gap between the learning and the doing. During that gap, some of the learning is lost. You aren't getting your money's worth if you don't arrange for quick application and repetition of the new skill.

4 *Feedback.* "How am I doing?" is a question to which everyone wants the answer. Not only do you provide the chance for the employee to practice or to apply the new knowledge and skill, you provide guidance and support through feedback. The more positive your feedback is, the better. If you are lacking the expertise that the employee demonstrates, if you can't really judge how well the employee is doing, get someone whose feedback will be relevant and valuable.

5 *Reinforcement of the new behavior.* When the practice and application are successful, don't forget: recognize, reinforce, reward. Once the new knowledge is well established, you can reinforce intermittently. But in the beginning, while the new behavior is being shaped, reinforce frequently.

Managers must be seen—and must see themselves —as primarily responsible for the effectiveness of the people who report to them. This is an unceasing and always varied task. The trainer is one resource working within an open, responsive system that the manager establishes. The learning should be equated with effectiveness; it should be continuing; it should be inductive as well as deductive to permit the learner to develop principles and concepts meaningful to him or her; it should be situational and directly related to the learner's needs; and finally, it should be rewarded.

17: A development tool that is a reward

At this point, I hope that you're thinking hard about specific approaches that can provide growth and development opportunities for the people who report to you, that can help you to satisfy your obligation as a manager to increase the effectiveness of subordinates—and thereby the effectiveness of the organization. In this chapter, I offer you an approach that is both a means and an end. That is, it provides the opportunity for your subordinates to expand their knowledge, to add to their experience, to learn new skills, to bolster their self-confidence. At the same time, the approach I'm about to describe can be used as a reward for good performance.

This tool is the task force.

Probably no other organizational form offers as much to the manager seeking more effective solutions to problems, more profitable decisions, more ways to explore and exploit opportunities, more effective methods to develop human resources, as the task force. The task force has almost universal relevance, if two premises are valid: First, most organizations, for one reason or another, have unresolved problems that, if confronted and worked through successfully, could materially contribute to the organization's well-being; and second, the human resources in no organization are continuously fully utilized.

Group approaches to problem solving are hardly new. There have always been staffs and committees. But for the most part these are advisory bodies subject to the authority of a higher manager who is free to accept or reject their deliberations and who has the real authority to act or not to act. In contrast, a task force has these characteristics:

It is formed to *accomplish* a specific task.

It is a *temporary* problem-solving group, with temporary authority and responsibility to do what is necessary to achieve its goal.

The group's responsibility extends beyond merely suggesting solutions or making recommendations. The true task force has responsibility for carrying out what it proposes. It *proposes and disposes.* Its work is not usually completed until its recommendations are adopted and found workable.

It is usually *interdepartmental,* or *interfunctional.* It cuts across departmental or functional boundaries (and barriers). It usually consists of people of varying backgrounds, experience, and disciplines.

The task force enjoys a high degree of *autonomy.* The group should be as free as possible to establish its schedule, methods of working, means of resolving the matter before it, and even in some situations to determine its own leadership.

The members of the temporary group should be *free from interference* by their regular managers while doing task-force work. The work of the group ideally should be placed under the umbrella of an executive powerful enough to provide protection for the group and to act as a source of authority.

Decisions should be made by *consensus* as much as possible. Majority rule too often leaves some participants dissatisfied, and lessens their commitment to those decisions. The members of a task force should all be able to agree that the solution they have reached is the best that could be found given the circumstances, and is superior to what any one member could achieve operating alone.

You can see readily from the above why the task force is no ordinary kind of assignment. There's a distinction to being asked to work on a problem or a project that the organization regards as important, and that, for one reason or another, individuals or organizational units have not been able to solve or in many cases to tackle. The distinction is heightened if the other members of the task force are also regarded as high performers. It is likely that each person in the group will enjoy more authority than he or she is accustomed to, simply because the group has been awarded greater latitude and power than would be available to members on their respective levels. The group wields more clout in presenting its solutions and recommendations to management. Participating on a task force brings high visibility with relatively low individual risk taking.

Problems—all sizes and shapes

The problems that a task force takes on may be large or small. For example, the managers of one division of a large corporation agreed that it would be useful to meet together for a weekend at a hotel away from the site of the division. Six managers were selected to make preparations. Meeting once or twice a week for three months, the group allocated the planning tasks among themselves, solicited the various departments for ideas, prepared an agenda for the meeting, and negotiated with the hotel. During the weekend meeting itself, the task force members, each responsible for a phase of the meeting, following their original allocation, kept it running smoothly.

On a much higher level, Company A was purchased by much larger Corporation B. The executives of the parent corporation were not happy with the management of the newly acquired subsidiary. Instead of replacing those managers, the corporate president came up with an innovative plan for keeping Company A going while its executives were having their skills up-graded. From the various divisions and subsidiary companies, the president selected promising managers who had good performance records and assigned them to a task force that would run Company A. During the up-grading period, policies were set by the task force. Each member of the group was assigned to an executive of Company A. Operating decisions were made jointly by A's executives and their corporate shadows, except, of course, when an executive of the subsidiary was away. Then the respective member of the management task force would be in charge completely. Gradually, with a minimum of replacement, the executives of Company A began to operate up to corporate standards, and the task force was dissolved. For its members, the assignment had been both a reward and a growth opportunity.

In the summer of 1967, I was asked to join a group of The Research Institute professionals to determine what could and should be done with *Report to Members*, a weekly publication that went to thousands of middle managers who had been enrolled by their organizations as members of the Institute. It was an important report. But it had no focus. What went into it was whatever copy was available. Members who received it would have been unable to say how it helped them to be effective managers. The subject matter this week might be financial and marketing, the next week administrative (procedures and policy), the following week something on managing people, etc. There was no theme, no consistency, no clearly defined objective.

For approximately a year I had been trying to contribute one article per week, chiefly having to do with sales management and marketing. It had been a frustrating experience, especially because editorial direction was limited or nonexistent. Finally, the managing editor was terminated, and *Report to Members* was put into the hands of the task force. My appointment to this group was, for me, a reward for all of the frustration and hard work of the year.

The members of the task force were truly interdisciplinary—a lawyer, an economist, a wage-and-hour-law specialist, two specialists in supervisory skills, a former salesman, etc. We designed our own leadership: Each member of the task force would, for two weeks, act as managing editor and, simultaneously, chairperson of the group. The others would contribute copy and editorial evaluation—each article would undergo criticism by all task force members. Although no member of the group was a specialist in what is now called organizational behavior, that was the focus decided upon for the publication. The reasoning was simple. Here was a weekly report going to controllers, plant managers, engineers, sales directors, etc. How could we keep the report pertinent to all of these people in differing functions? The one thing they had in common was behavior —theirs, subordinates', colleagues', managers'. They shared a concern for effective behavior and interpersonal skills.

Gradually the content of *Report to Members* began to reveal this new thrust—how to be more effective in dealing with others. The feedback from other Institute professionals and from members was positive. The gratifying response confirmed our judgment.

Before disbanding, the task force recommended that two of its members be editorially responsible for the refurbished publication. (I was one of the two.) Until a larger staff could be assembled, members of the task force pledged to continue their contributions.

It was a successful group effort, more so than we had imagined during those five months of 1967. *Report to Members* eventually became *Personal Report for the Executive,* one of the most profitable Institute publications, and probably the most widely read publication of its kind. For me, the reward has never stopped rewarding.

Most managers would have no difficulty finding problems or projects for a task force to work on. Some thought-starters: designing a training program; introducing a new product, a merchandising or marketing plan; changing procedures or work flow; reorganizing a department or a function; establishing work methods for groups that must collaborate; deciding on a capital investment. Almost any problem, large or small, is suitable for a task force, which can indeed turn it into an opportunity.

Seeing how decisions are made

Managers often find that projects which involve the participation of several functions can get off the ground more quickly when they are entrusted to a task force. When all the parties interested in the project participate at the same time, decision making proceeds at a brisker pace than does the slower, repetitious, sequential decision making usually encountered in organizations. And task-force members have a chance to observe their own decision-making processes, the purest form of learning by doing.

For example, the R & D department of Xerxes Corporation designs a potential new product that arouses the enthusiasm of top management. Under its prodding, the engineering department goes to work to find out what facilities and processes would be required to produce it. Modifications are suggested to make the production more feasible and the cost more competitive. R & D changes its design.

Now Production takes a look at what has emerged from R & D and Engineering, and complains that it does not have the right people. So there is a delay while it is determined what skills are needed and while recruiting goes on for people with those skills.

Then, Distribution reports that its traditional channels aren't entirely suitable for the new product. And

Sales holds everything up to study whether the present field sales force is competent to handle the new load or if expansion is necessary. The entire cycle may have to be undertaken again. The chief problem is that each department's decisions reflected its concern for its own welfare and its limited interpretation of the total organizational needs.

A task force can avoid these pitfalls because its decision making involves the desired technical knowledge and familiarity with the respective functions, allows for tentative testing of the decisions made at each step, and encourages the commitment of each of the functions to the group actions, because each of the functions has participated in the project as a whole.

For you, the task force approach to making decisions has, aside from training people in skills, a substantial advantage: the consensus decision. Most managers experienced in using task forces prefer consensus decisions that all members of the group can accept without serious reservations. Getting consensus can be slower than resorting to majority vote or unilateral decisions. But the slowness—and thoroughness—produces valuable benefits:

Everyone's views are aired, interests surface. No one feels left out.

The decision is one that everyone identifies with. It's not a compromise, where everyone has to give up something (usually what they most want). In a consensus, one who has participated in making the decision feels it is the best that could have been made.

People who have made a consensus decision are committed to it. They can't withdraw—it represents their best efforts. They don't "just go along." They have a real desire to *prove* that their decision is a good one.

True consensus decisions often are better than the best decision offered by any one member.

The task force and training

Many managers express dissatisfaction with traditional approaches to training and development. And they have reasons. To cite a few:

> Many training and development techniques are regarded by managers (or trainees) as involving contingencies that may or may not occur; the content does not relate to their perceived needs.

> Much management development involves simulations that pose little or no risk to the learner. Indeed, the most tangible and immediate rewards in performing simulations will derive not from learning principles but from "beating" the game design or others in competitive groups.

> Vast portions of education offered managers for their growth do not relate to the individual's talents, capacity, interest, or career direction. They are off-the-shelf or prepackaged.

> Continuing education for managers leans in the academic direction. More planning should be undertaken to provide empirical learning, in which managers can absorb what they feel is most helpful to them in an environment and under conditions that closely resemble those in which they are expected to work and grow.

Consequently, many experts on learning today favor educational programs that relate closely to the *individual's* perception of needs. When a manager recognizes a need to have a skill or certain knowledge, he or she will attach more value to acquiring it. For example, if a manager attends a course on budgeting, the chances are that if he knows he will be responsible for his department's budget in the months ahead, he will invest far more of himself in the learning experiences than if he is simply preparing for some time in the future when he might be asked to take over the budgeting function.

Assess the task force experience in light of these

learning theories or assumptions. For most managers, the situation that prompts the formation of the task force will have novel and challenging aspects, both in the problem or decision to be explored and in the inter-personal relations. It will probably be a risk-taking in-volvement, in that the manager's efforts on behalf of the task force are public, for other members to see. If task-force members' performances are to be evaluated, then they have a very definite stake in the outcome of the group efforts; each one wants the group to "win." The task force has a real work environment just as the de-partments from which its members have come. If the leadership is effective, the manager will have frequent opportunities to contribute special skills and qualities and to measure his relative lack of skill in various areas. And, working in an environment in which trust levels are higher than those in other environments, managers acquire a more reliable picture of their performance through feedback from others on the task force. Finally, the manager on a task force can see the consequences of what he or she has been doing, an essential step in learning that is often denied in organizational settings.

Job enrichment

Until recently, there seems to have been reluctance to acknowledge the possibility that managers can become bored or restless, feel "dead-ended," or otherwise have little sense of growth and progress. When managers on the task force are working on problems or toward deci-sions that they usually would not have responsibility for, and when they are acting—within the group—with authority and power that are normally not vested in them, and confronting risk that, individually, they would not ordinarily be expected to deal with, then par-ticipation in a task force clearly is an enrichment of the job. In the language of Frederick Herzberg, it is vertical loading. (Indeed, the task force experience can be so heady that managers sometimes complain of a letdown on returning to regular functions after the group has accomplished its objectives.)

Utilizing the underutilized

There are other kinds of organizational—and people— needs that task forces can help to meet.

First, there are the shelf-sitters and nonpromotables. The dynamism of an organization is severely crippled when career paths are choked with managers who cannot be promoted because of limited ability, who are in effect waiting out the last year or two until retirement, or who are uninterested in moving further up but resist being shunted aside. Still, these people wouldn't be where they are if they didn't have considerable abilities, so one answer is to put them to work on a group project, thereby using that ability and at the same time opening up the formal vertical paths to younger aspirants. That way, everyone feels rewarded (especially you).

Some organizations have also been successful in using task forces to help resolve the embarrassing problem of the manager who has been raised above his level of competence. To demote him or fire him might be too drastic, but if he were assigned to a team project more in keeping with his skills and experience, he might be able to save face (as would the executive who promoted him) and make a real contribution besides.

Task forces can also meet the organizational need for a management reservoir. Keeping a talented and ambitious person happy and challenged until there is a slot to which he or she can be promoted is a tough job, especially as the manager moves higher toward the peak of the pyramid, where opportunities thin out. An organization that uses task forces has the opportunity to keep that person in a learning situation, to keep the manager laterally mobile. It probably won't work forever, but task force assignments can at least slow attrition.

Simply assigning more work to a valued employee may be seen by you as a recognition of that value, but that view is not always shared by the subordinate. The work should be meaningful, and challenging. It should provide more visibility to the employee. If possible, the task should be significantly different from everyday responsibilities. A well-designed task force meets these qualifications. That is why such problem-solving groups can be a potent element among your rewards for good performance.

18: What makes a good boss?

Not long ago, after a speech I had given, a member of the audience asked me this question: "For what kind of a boss do you think you would work well?" What follows is an expanded version of my answer.

The kind of person I would prefer to report to, and with whom I feel I could most effectively work, would:

1 *Give me space.* I don't want a boss who is constantly looking over my shoulder, checking on me. Such a manager conveys the message, "I don't trust you to work, or to work well, if I am not around." This, by the way, is a prevalent fear among managers whose organizations are instituting flexible work schedules—flextime, for example. Some of the employees will come in before the manager gets to work, or will be working after the boss goes home. Some supervisors, I'm told, are tempted, in the beginning, to work eleven- or twelve-hour days, because they believe that subordinates will either goof off or flounder when the boss is not there. They soon discover, in most cases, that the work gets done as it does when they are there, monitoring in person. My preferred boss has confidence that I shall do the work according to his or her standards, even when I am working alone and without being checked.

However, this does not mean that I want to be entirely without supervision or direction. I don't want to work in a vacuum. I need to know what I am supposed to do, and how well I am expected to do it. Thus, I require periodic conferences with the boss. During these discussions the manager says, in effect, "These are the things we have to accomplish. This is your part of it. These are the standards and the schedules we must observe." Then the manager leaves me, to the extent possible, to do my job.

2 *Expect me to have goals—and to need them.* Therefore, the manager will sit down with me from time to time to make sure I am getting what I want from the job, so far as is possible. When I say that I want a boss who cares about me, this is the caring I mean. My manager, through these discussions, is giving me the type of consideration that I am sure he or she wants from higher management. The manager recognizes that I have certain needs that can be met through work—as probably nowhere else. And he or she is interested in my having these needs met, if it is possible to do so.

3 *Answer my question, "How am I doing?"* If I suspect that I am not working effectively, not getting the results I should be getting, I want to know that, painful as it may be to hear. For one thing, the work I do is as important to me as it is to the organization—and in many cases to my co-workers as well. For another, when things are not going well, and I sense that fact, I experience tension. That tension will prevent me from working as I ought to and wish to. I want to have results and to take pride in the work. The manager ensures both when he or she steps in when I perform less than effectively.

By the same token, I need to know when I have performed well. Or I may feel it inside, but I want to know that others recognize it. I don't want to be taken for granted. I will suspect that I am if I never or seldom hear that I am doing a good piece of work.

If I am working in a better than average way, I want a pat on the back, a good word. Praise that is genuine is something of which I never grow weary. But I know

that there are other ways a manager can reward me.
Not money. I like it, but I know that salary policies are
set by staff administrators, not managers. Thus, I'm not
going to get as much money as I think I deserve. But
there are ways, little and big, that a manager can say,
"I appreciate the work you are doing." I regret it,
maybe even resent it, when my manager gets too busy
or complacent to think of ways to get that message
across to me.

4 *Know I want to grow.* It's true that I get a lot of
satisfaction from the work I do day to day. But my
enthusiasm won't be very high if I suspect that, three
years from now, I'll be doing essentially the same thing.
I want to know that, in three to five years, even to some
extent next year, I'll be capable of doing things that I
can't do now. Or able to do things more easily or better
than now.

Therefore, it's important to me to have a boss ask,
"What do you want to do with the rest of your life?
Where do you want to go?" I don't require that my boss
do my life/career planning for me. Sometimes the boss
can't advise or help me. But in asking important questions about what I want to do with my life, my manager
is showing how much I am valued. If the boss did not
value me, it's unlikely that the questions would ever get
asked.

5 *Make the job exciting.* I respect a manager who
sees as an obligation making the work exciting for
subordinates. It's not that difficult to do. As a boss, you
help to make the work meaningful by showing me that
it is important to the overall work and objectives of the
organization; helping me to set goals so that I can have
a sense, a clear record, of achievement; and by matching
the work I do, if possible, with what you suspect are my
personal goals, with what you observe turns me on. Not
only do you make the work significant and exciting, you
create in me expectation of reward: "Do a good job, and
I'll find a way to reward you."

I like to have the feeling of getting up in the morning and anticipating the day. I look forward to getting to work, because I like the prospect of fun, excitement, challenge, and achievement. At the end of the day, if things go right, I shall value myself even more than I do in the morning.

The manager is the key

Those are some managerial qualities and behaviors that I regard as very important. There is another quality that may be even more important: respect. You may like your subordinates, but liking or affection is not terribly important. What is essential is respect. You respect them by accepting that they have goals, aspirations, needs, as you have them. Not necessarily the same ones (projecting his or her own values and needs onto subordinates is one of the most serious mistakes a manager can make). Your respect for them will go a long way toward forming the base for their respect for you.

I can't emphasize too strongly that there must be respect between a manager and subordinates. A manager must be credible. If you say that you will do something, people need to believe that, barring unforeseen circumstances and those beyond your control, you will do it. Respect and credibility are absolutely necessary in motivation management: Good work will be recognized. No exceptions.

But you get busy. From time to time, you may be preoccupied with putting out fires. And you have your relationships with your boss and higher management to build and maintain. Perhaps you feel aggrieved that your own boss is not always consistent in recognizing your performance. You are human, and thus, you need to be reminded:

You are the key to the productivity of subordinates.

There is no message in this book that is more important. In fact, it is the justification of this book.

I am under no illusion that following the steps I have outlined in this book will make you a perfect manager. They will help you to be a more respected manager. Not loved, necessarily, or even liked, but respected and trusted by your subordinates on whom you depend. The techniques in this book will help you to get more of the results you want. Because you will be dealing with adult human beings in an adult respectful manner. Just as important, you will be helping them to get what they want out of their working life by investing their energies in helping you to get what you want.

What many managers would be unwilling to admit about themselves is that they very often manage for personal gratification. They like to exercise power for the feeling of having it. Or they want to be liked by subordinates. Or they find that they are good at organizational politics, and how they manage employees depends largely upon how those employees can strengthen the manager's political power and status.

Noting the reasons why managers manage the way they do could create a very long list. But there is really only one good reason for management: to get the desired results—for the organization, for the manager, for the employees. Everything else is secondary, or perhaps even obstructive.

A good example of what I am saying was the late George Szell, for many years the musical director of the Cleveland Orchestra. Szell wanted results, and he spared no efforts to get them. Szell also knew that the one hundred or so musicians who played in the orchestra wanted results. They all wanted to produce good music. They wanted to be superior musicians, and to be regarded as such by the rest of the world. There is no question that Szell saw himself as a superior person. I'm sure that he wanted everyone else to see him as superior as he saw himself.

But the result was fine music, or even great music, delivered in a great manner.

That's what counted. Szell apparently had no real interest in being liked. Most people who have written about George Szell describe him, personally, in unflattering terms. And he was an autocrat in dealing with members of the orchestra, which has some implications for those management experts who feel that a democratic, participative style is necessarily the best. (I favor such a style for myself, but I will not preach it as the best for everyone.)

Szell, working with his musicians, built one of the greatest orchestras in the world. The *esprit* of the orchestra was high, even fierce. A guest conductor is reported to have said, "I felt as if I were facing one hundred Szells when I stepped on the podium."

Performance was on a consistently high level. And there was plenty of gratification for everyone. It came because everyone connected with the Cleveland Orchestra was getting results, was achieving what was important to him or her.

If everyone in any kind of organization remembered that—results come when people are achieving what is important to them—there is no doubt in my mind that productivity, which seems to be such a serious problem in this country, would increase enormously, would soar.

The answer, as I indicated at the outset, is motivation. The manager who knows how to unblock, to free, to enhance the motivating forces in the people who report to him or her knows how to get performance results —superior performance results.

Index